THE
COMEBACK

The role that won nothing but trouble: Jay Robinson as the mad emperor—
Caligula. (Photo courtesy of Twentieth Century-Fox.)

THE COMEBACK

JAY ROBINSON

as told to Jim Hardiman

Published by

√chosen books

Lincoln, Virginia 22078

Distributed by Word Books • Waco, Texas 76703

Scripture quotations identified NEB are from the New English Bible, © The Delegates of the Oxford University Press and The Syndics of The Cambridge University Press, 1961, 1970 and are reprinted by permission. All other Scripture quotations are from the King James Version of the Bible.

Photos from *The Robe* and *Demetrius and the Gladiators* (pp. 2, 86) are courtesy of Twentieth Century-Fox. *The Robe,* copyright © 1953 Twentieth Century-Fox Film Corp. All Rights reserved. *Demetrius and the Gladiators,* © 1954.

Library of Congress Cataloging in Publication Data

Robinson, Jay, 1930–
The comeback.

1. Robinson, Jay, 1930–   2. Converts—United States—Biography. I. Hardiman, James W., joint author.
II. Title.
BV4935.R573A32   248'.24 [B]   78–31489

ISBN 0-912376-45-7

To Pauline

Contents

Foreword by Bette Davis   9

1   Caligula   11
2   A Boy's Dreams   19
3   Broadway   26
4   Two Life-Changing Words   37
5   Emperor of Hollywood   44
6   Star Treatment   53
7   Downhill in a Gold Cadillac   61
8   Reunion   70
9   Descent into Hell   75
10 Enter Pauline   89
11 Monkey off My Back   95
12 Comeback Begun   103
13 Journey to the Past   112
14 Broadway Revisited   123
15 Crisis at Saranac Lake   129
16 The Prodigal Returns   136
17 Three Minutes to Say Good-by   145
18 "The Big House"   164

19   At the Gladiator School   169
20   Easter Sunday   177
21   Caligula Returns   184
22   Fire Fighter   191
23   The Glass Mountain   203
24   Persistence and Determination   209
25   Sudden Change   221
26   Return to Chino   232
Epilogue   239
Afterword by Charles Colson   243
Acknowledgments   247
Stage, Screen, and Television Appearances   249

"The Comeback" is a book about a very talented actor, Jay Robinson. This talent was ever present during those years that were black. The "Comeback," even if you never heard of Jay Robinson, is a powerful story of a man who survived those years and finally, by getting to know God, found a new life.

Let us hail him and let us hail his wife Pauline, who, because she really loved him, stuck with him through those black years and never gave up trying to prove to him his way to salvation was through God. Who, she devoutly believed was always available for help to those who asked for his help.

This belief finally made Jay's Comeback possible.

Congratulations Jay for an inspirational book for one and all who "fall by the way side"

January 20, 1979   Bette Davis

1

Caligula

THE HOUR HAS COME.

The people of Rome hunger for blood in the Coliseum. And I, Gaius Caesar, will see that they get it.

I arise slowly from my couch, suppressing a groan. A slave helps me into my purple toga. Then the gold-wreathed crown is gently placed on my regal head. Another slave bows low and pulls back the huge cyprus door to my private passageway leading to the Coliseum.

For an instant I hesitate at the door. The tunnel-like corridor is dark with ghostly shadows. Its stone walls are dank and the clammy air is fetid with the smell of death and decay.

I must not show my fear of the dark. Am I not the Emperor of all men? Do not millions cower at my feet?

I step through the door. My head throbs and my stomach is queasy from the assault of last night's revels. But I am Emperor. Why should I suffer the same as a wine-sotted servant? Am I not a god?

Straightening my shoulders, I stride forward. My golden leather boots from which I derive my nickname, Caligula, slap the damp pavement stones in steady, rhythmic cadence.

Around me like a living wall of armor gather my faithful Praetorian Guard. The passageway echoes to the clanking of their swords, the heavy rustle of their leather armor and solid stomp of marching feet. It is nonsense for me to be afraid, for these men exist only to protect my imperial person.

The shadowy corridor curves before me, seemingly to infinity. Beads of moisture clinging to the rough hewn blocks of granite reflect the orange flame of sputtering torches suspended by iron brackets along the walls.

I am startled by the sight of two beady eyes glittering at me from the darkness. But it is only a rat, and it scuttles away into the gloom.

On our left looms another passage, and my trusty Praetorians swing into it without losing pace. It is guarded by a lone Praetorian standing rigidly at attention. As I pass he slaps his sword over his heart in salute, the shaft thundering against his breastplate, the noise reverberating into the distance.

The tunnel floor now slopes up toward a brilliant square of light. As we approach the sunlight, warmth gradually invades the dankness. The commander barks an order and a leading guardsman doubles forward into the Coliseum to announce my approach.

A thousand golden trumpets are raised skyward, silken banners emblazoned with the Imperial eagle fluttering from each one. Strident notes fill the air in a crescendoing fanfare for their emperor.

I draw my cloak tighter over my shoulder, lift my head with its crown of golden laurel leaves, and stride forward into the blazing sunlight. I am engulfed in a sea of light and sound that washes over me like ocean surf. I am nearly blinded by the brilliance of a summer Rome sun, but as my eyes adjust to the light I see a hundred thousand Romans who have sprung to their feet at the first sound of the trumpets. Then comes a roar from a hundred thousand throats: "HAIL CAESAR! HAIL CAESAR! HAIL CAESAR!" The intoxicating sound fills me with sensual satisfaction.

As I soak up the idolatry of the Roman mob, I am beyond fear now. And my physical sickness has vanished too. For now I am a god supported by my faithful. I am Caligula! I am the God Emperor! I am Rome, center of the world, and its king!

I stop for a moment to acknowledge the adulation, then settle onto my throne beneath the carved, gold eagle. The shouts subside, but there is an electric air of expectancy.

The parade of the gladiators begins. Sun glints off polished brass, silver and gold armor. Drums beat a hypnotic vibration and the brass horns sound an accolade to heroes. Again the mob erupts into a thunderous roar of approval, but this time the sound displeases me. How dare they salute Caesar and these crude men in the same manner? As I study the gladiators, I can visualize their spilled blood and vow they will pay dearly for the mob's applause.

The combatants halt before me, swords raised in salute. Their voices chant in unison: "Hail Caesar. We who are about to die salute you." Their salute mollifies me and my anger subsides.

Imperiously I wave my arm. "Let the games begin."

But today the fighting is poor and I soon tire of it; my mind wanders. The face of the gladiator now in the arena reminds me of Demetrius. I bite my lower lip at the memory of what happened in the slave market just before I was made emperor. A Greek had stepped up on the block, a man of heroic build and in wonderful physical condition. He delighted me in every way. I knew he was a Christian, and while this sect was beginning to irritate me, it was of no consequence. This Greek was a superb man. And I intended to have him.

I had leaned over to my chief aide, Tribune Quintus. "Buy him."

Quintus made his bid, his voice loud to carry into every corner of the market. Everyone knew he was bidding for me, the chosen of the gods who would ascend the throne and be master of all Romans.

I licked my lips in anticipation.

And then Tribune Marcellus Gallio, seated nearby, arose. "One hundred," he called.

Gasps of surprise ran through the market and all turned to stare at Marcellus. Surely he would not publicly defy me.

My heart pounded with rage. "You bid against ME?" I hissed across the short space separating us.

Marcellus pretended not to understand my sudden outburst. "No, Sire, against Tribune Quintus."

The bidding continued. "One hundred and fifty gold pieces," said Quintus.

"Two hundred," replied Marcellus.

Back and forth it went until I leaned forward and declared: "Five hundred!"

There could be no other bidding for the Greek. I, Caligula, was now speaking.

Still Marcellus did not hesitate. "Six hundred."

"One thousand."

Finally the bid was raised to the impossible price of three thousand gold pieces. I glared at the insolent Marcellus, fury pulsing through my body.

Resolved not to take any further part in this charade, I had sat motionless on my throne, my intestines churning, my brow beaded with sweat.

"Sold to Tribune Gallio for three thousand pieces of gold," announced the auctioneer.

My ears had buzzed with madness as I stared at Marcellus in blind hatred. If I could, I would have killed him on the spot.

Gradually I became aware that the buzzing in my ears was real. It came from the mob at the arena before me and drew me back from the hateful memories.

A bout had apparently just ended and a defeated gladiator lay flat on his back in the dirt. The sword point of the victor was poised at his throat awaiting my command. Every eye in the arena was directed toward me. Was he to live or die?

Apparently it had been a good bout for the overwhelming cries of the crowd were for mercy. I looked at the warrior lying there, his gaze fixed on me in a silent plea for life. As I stared back, his features took on the appearance of Demetrius, follower of that Jewish upstart, Jesus. I felt myself filled anew with fury.

My renewed humiliation at the memory of the slave market sealed the fallen gladiator's fate. I extended my right arm before me, straight out from my shoulder, and slowly, with great deliberation, savoring the full taste of victory, turned my thumb downward.

The crowd sucked in its collective breath in a great sigh of dismay. Some bleats of protest were raised but quickly stifled. I sat back, filled with satisfaction as the sword sank deeply into the throat of the fallen gladiator. Bright red blood surged upward and fell to the arena floor where it was quickly swallowed by the hot sand.

I am the greatest god of all! This Jesus with his puny band of followers was not equal to a platoon of Roman legionnaires. I am Caligula, the all-powerful. How I savored the imposition of my will over that of the mob!

"CUT. . . . PRINT IT." The voice of my director dragged me rudely forward nearly two thousand years in a matter of seconds, into the twentieth century with its freeways and jet planes. I found myself no longer the Emperor Caligula but the actor I was in real life, Jay Robinson.

At the director's signal, the Romans filling the arena relaxed into the $25-a-day extras they really were, producing copies of the *Hollywood Reporter* or *Daily Variety* out of mysterious hidden recesses in their costumed togas. Many lit cigarettes in a most un-Roman manner. Women extras whipped out pocketbooks and applied fresh lipstick or combed out their hair from the effects of the wind and sun. The Praetorians guarding me sauntered off as if I no longer existed, probably to the men's room or the coffee urn that the union said had to be on the set.

The "dead" gladiator got up and walked off toward the dressing rooms, accompanied by a makeup man who wiped away the imitation blood with a purple towel.

The studio crew, dressed in blue jeans and sports shirts, scuttled around setting up for the next take as I tried to bridge the gap between reality and my still-fresh fantasy. In my mind I was still Caligula, the anti-Christ. The camera had stopped rolling, but I could not turn my head off that quickly. I was no machine. For as a good actor, I had absorbed the character I played.

Soon I would return to my own imperial palace I had created in that modern-day Roman suburb of Bel Air where I could enjoy orgies of my own.

The Robe was a huge success and made me a star. And, as a movie star, I was an emperor. And like the Caligula I played, I felt invincible!

The epic *Demetrius and the Gladiators* immediately followed *The Robe* in production as Twentieth Century Fox used the same sets. Again I was Caligula, Roman Emperor and motion picture star. At the end of a day's shooting, I was surrounded by my own Praetorian guard of Hollywood hangers-on and studio employees. They flanked me and brought up the rear as I swept through the studio streets dressed in the flowing scarlet and gold robes of Caligula. They followed me in through the arched doorway of the studio building and on up the red carpeted staircase to the second floor door on which my name was affixed to a gold, five-pointed star.

Inside my suite, my feet sank almost to the ankles in the luxury of deep wall-to-wall carpeting. Lighting was subtle and indirect, highlighting sofa, armchairs and other comfortable furnishings. Soft background music floated from hi-fi speakers around the room. Only the rows of white lights glaring around my makeup mirror disturbed the otherwise discreet atmosphere, harshly revealing the jumble of pots, jars, tubes and all the paraphernalia of makeup on the table before it.

Quickly my makeup artist helped me remove the layers of heavy pancake made necessary by the new Cinemascope anamorphic lenses. My hairdresser washed out the sprayings that had held my hair rigidly coiffed all day long in a ringlet of curls within the encircling gold crown of Caligula. The dresser helped me doff the robes of a Roman emperor and don my own casually elegant garments.

As they worked, a studio publicist discussed upcoming interviews, personal appearances and photo sessions, while my secretary got my approval for appointments requested that day and reminded me of those scheduled for the following day.

The second assistant director knocked discreetly at my dressing room door, handing my secretary the "call" sheet for the following day and left with a respectful, "Good night, Mr. Robinson."

"You have an early call again, Mr. Robinson," my secretary informed me. "Six-thirty for makeup and wardrobe, and an eight o'clock shooting call on stage 15."

I groaned aloud, letting those present feel the awful responsibility of being a star. Secretly I enjoyed every single second of it, relishing my name and face everywhere in the press, on television and soon to be on countless theatre fronts across the nation.

Now I was dressed for the street in a chocolate brown Italian silk shirt, light tan gabardine slacks and Gucci loafers and belt, all accented by gold accessories, rings and a gold wristwatch.

By the time I reached the front door of the studio building, my secretary already had my gold plated Cadillac convertible gently purring at the curb.

As I slid into the driver's seat it was past seven o'clock and evening shadows were lengthening upon the sidewalk. I had been at the studio since sunup, almost thirteen hours before. But as my Fox contract paid me the princely salary of $3,000 a week, I did not resent the long hours.

The guard at the studio gate gave me a straight-arm salute— "Goodnight, Mr. Robinson"—while two young starlets, revealing a great deal through summer slacks and halter tops, giggled and tossed me provocative waves. Their eyes spoke eloquent invitations, promising an evening of fun to equal any ancient Roman reveling. But I had no time tonight. Marilyn Monroe, James Dean, Debbie Reynolds, Natalie Wood, Robert Wagner, Jeff Hunter and others were coming to a party at my new Bel Air mansion.

I turned my Cadillac across Santa Monica and Wilshire Boulevards toward Sunset Boulevard.

The majestic gates of Bel Air beckoned me toward my home where a private guard patrol, within its secluded preserve, protected neighbors such as Gary Cooper, Humphrey Bogart and Lauren Bacall, Bing Crosby, Zsa Zsa Gabor, Tyrone Power and Jean Simmons. And now I lived among them, the half-Jewish kid who had arrived from Florida on a bus such a short time ago, armed with nothing more than a dauntless ego and a will to succeed.

I drove through the narrow, twisting, country-like lanes of the private kingdom of Bel Air toward my palace set in a tropical rain forest of my own creation. As I nosed the Cadillac into my driveway I could hear the chatter from the enormous cages full of monkeys and apes I maintained on the grounds.

I walked into the living room, where an actual waterfall flowed, and then into the banquet hall. Mike Romanoff, the celebrated prince of caterers, was putting the final touches to my imperial buffet adorned with orchids and floral displays. An illuminated fountain of champagne was being tested as I swept on toward my master bedroom suite with its magnificent dark brown velvet bedspread with the imperial gold laurel wreath embroidered on its center. I considered a luxurious bath in my elegant sunken tub, then decided against it.

There was barely time to wash my face before the first guests arrived for the Roman evening to which they had been summoned. As I dried my hands on golden towels bearing the Emperor's insignia, I heard the entrance chimes peal. I straightened myself, preened for a moment before the mirror, then strode toward the living room and the forthcoming revels.

Caligula was at home and would be pleased to welcome guests.

2

A Boy's Dream

FROM EARLIEST CHILDHOOD I remember yearning for affection
and attention. But my parents, trapped by their own frustrations,
couldn't respond. I think their marriage was in trouble even before
I was born on April 14, 1930. Probably it was because they had
so little in common.

My father, Stanley Robinson, was of Jewish heritage. He was
one of the founders and a director of the Van Heusen Company,
then the country's largest shirt manufacturer. He was also the chief
designer and stylist for the firm. A handsome, athletic man with
dark wavy hair, he had a gruff manner that hid a soft heart.

My mother, Barbara Breslaw Robinson, had a Presbyterian background. She had been a famous dancer in Broadway musical comedies in the 1920s. Known as Bobbie Breslaw, she appeared with
many of the big Broadway stars of that era. Earlier she had been
a member of the New York Metropolitan Opera Corps de Ballet.
Her honey-blonde hair framed a heart-shaped face, while her tiny,
cupid's-bow mouth and expressive, large blue eyes made her completely bewitching. She was like a porcelain doll come to life. Outgo-
ing and exuberant, she loved attending parties, plays and musicals.
But childlike, she wasn't sure just how to relate to the little boy
born to her.

Neither of my parents went to church, nor was religion ever
discussed in our home.

When I was a small child we lived in an apartment at a Central Park West address in New York City. I recall Dad always sitting in his chair during the evening, smoking cigars and reading the newspaper or financial reports. Mother would chafe and complain about his wanting to spend so much time at home. When I asked Mother to read to me, she would send me to Dad. He would pat me on the head, read one story, turn back to his paper and send me back to Mother. I felt like a ball being tossed back and forth.

Some of the stories Dad did read to me were about puppies. I felt sure they loved little boys. One day in front of our apartment building a woman accidentally let go of the leash of her little dog. The fluffy little thing scampered over to me and began licking my face. I put my arms around the small dog hugging it.

Mother pulled me away, scolding, but my heart was lost. I turned my attention to animals, absorbing everything about them I could find. The autumn I was four I asked if I could have a puppy for Christmas. When my parents agreed, I was ecstatic and began dreaming of the fun of having a little dog.

One night a few days before Christmas I was on my way to bed when I heard my parents talking in their bedroom.

"I just can't see us with a dog messing up the apartment," said Mother.

"Jay will take care of him," replied my father.

"But he's too young to feed him and clean up after him."

I stood in the hall frozen.

"Why not give it a try?" I could sense it was my father's final effort on my behalf.

"I'm afraid it won't work," she said. "I'll be the one who will have to take care of it."

"Jay will be terribly disappointed."

"He'll get over it," she said, then added enthusiastically: "I know! Let's give him a big stuffed dog."

My father was silent for a moment. "All right, I'll tell Jay that the apartment manager will no longer allow people in this building to keep dogs."

"That's a good way to handle it."

The next evening Dad called me over to his chair. Putting down his cigar, he pulled a letter from his pocket. "Jay, I have bad news for you. Here's a letter from the manager of this apartment building. He says we're not allowed to have dogs here anymore. Shall I read it to you?"

I fled to my room and sobbed on the bed for the rest of the evening. I loved my parents, but my respect for them was tarnished from then on.

Conflicts between Mother and Dad grew so sharp that they were divorced in 1935. A year later they remarried. But when I was seven they divorced a second time. It was traumatic for me because I really didn't understand what was happening. All I knew was that my beautiful mother was unhappy and my handsome father sat glowering in his chair each evening, puffing up clouds of smoke from a cigar that glowed fiery red.

After the second divorce, Mother and I left New York to live with my maternal grandmother, Etta MacDonald Breslaw, in Miami Beach. We moved into a two-story house on Hibiscus Island. It was a lovely home overlooking the bay, with four bedrooms, rose gardens and grassy terraces.

Like a butterfly finding a new flower garden, Mother became completely absorbed in the social life of Miami Beach. So Grandmother, a devout and affectionate Scottish Presbyterian lady, took over the rearing of one confused 7-year-old. Delighted with her new charge, she read the Bible to me, taught me to love flowers and helped me find solace through pets. Instead of one little puppy I was allowed to have two!

Grandmother also had a library and one afternoon while browsing through it I found my mother's scrapbook containing all her notices and photos. Fascinated, I spent hours poring over it, impressed by the adulation given my mother. Obviously, people loved her. It was then I decided to be an actor. In acting I saw that I too could project my frustrated personality. And in the theatre I sensed that loving waves of applause would wash back at me across the footlights.

By the time I was 11, two little neighborhood girls and I teamed up in an act in which we sang and danced to a current hit, *Chattanooga Choo Choo*. World War II had started and we put on a show in Miami Beach each evening for the USO. Our soldier audiences and their enthusiastic response convinced me that this was the way to earn the affection of others that I craved.

That same year Paramount Pictures announced a nationwide talent hunt to find a juvenile to play Gregory Peck and Jane Wyman's son in a film titled *The Yearling*. My longing to be an actor was now strong. I begged Mother to arrange an appointment to talk to their representative when he visited Miami. It was my first theatrical interview, but the part went to a young unknown, Claude Jarman, Jr. The film was a big hit, but it became my first theatrical disappointment.

During this time I began to live in a fantasy world where I assumed various roles that interested me. At the age of 12 one of my school chums was an English boy named Monty Steinhart. His accent so intrigued me that I copied it. Soon I imagined I was an English lad and was able to rapidly switch from a high class prep schooler to a poor boy with a cockney accent.

When I learned French in junior high school, I decided to become a French boy. To practice my dialect, I went to a small store featuring aquarium products run by two kindly Cuban ladies. I greeted them with a burst of French. They looked bewildered, but I noticed that I had won their attention and respect. From then on every time they saw me, their greeting was, "Here's the French boy." I gloated in the deception!

My hunger for affection must have been too much for my first two puppies. Both died. Grief-stricken, I turned to other animals, finally settling on monkeys after a visit to the Monkey Jungle just south of Miami.

But animals did not satisfy the yearning deep inside me to be truly loved for myself. And every time I found a person I cared for, I was rejected. At age 14 I went to dancing school and was dazzled by my striking, dark-haired dancing teacher named Pat. She was 18, very feminine, and taught me the rumba, tango and the samba. The warmth of her lithe, graceful body stimulated all my masculine instincts. I used every trick I knew to be with her and spent every cent I had on dancing lessons.

Pat was kind to me and enjoyed the worshiping attention I gave her. My fantasy world went wild with dreams of Pat and me being married and making a great hit as an acting and dancing team. When I got up the nerve to tell her what a great theatrical team we could be, she simply smiled and rumpled my hair.

Early one evening I went to the dance studio just as Pat was leaving on a date. Not wanting to be seen, I pulled back into the shadows. When the handsome young man pawed over "my" Pat as he helped her into his convertible, I gritted my teeth. But then came the crusher. The young man climbed behind the wheel of the car and must have said something funny. Pat laughed uproariously. Then she flung her arms around his neck. For a long moment they kissed. I slunk away, disillusioned and heartsick.

Letters from my father—most containing a five-dollar bill—brightened my life to some extent. He had remarried but still found time to visit me about twice a year. He would stay about a week in a nearby hotel and we would spend the days running together on the hot sands of the beach. At night he'd take me out for charcoal-broiled steak and prime rib dinners. During these times I'd almost forget my sadness over my parents' divorce and other disappointments.

But one day a letter came from him which grieved me deeply. He and his new wife had their own baby son. I felt further removed from my father.

Grandmother Breslaw was my main source of comfort during this period. Small in size for my age, I suffered numerous humiliations at the Miami Beach public schools, including bullying by rowdies. The fact that I skipped a grade twice in the first eight didn't help either. But when I would come limping home from school, Grandmother would apply ointment to the bruises and soothing words to my troubled spirit.

Yet Grandmother Breslaw also was separated from her husband, which made me wonder: do husbands and wives ever stay together? My grandfather was a kind but shadowy figure. I remember him as a learned man who talked about music, art and classical literature. Christmas Eve he had a stroke. We visited him in the hospital on Christmas Day and I was shocked at how terrible he looked. He died that night.

Grandmother was the one who introduced me to God, but He, too, became a vague and shadowy figure to me. Then during my early teens, Grandmother began to have stomach pains. A robust woman who rode horses and loved to work with her hands in the garden, it shocked me to see her turn very pale and stay in bed all day. Months passed. Finally, she had to be taken to the hospital.

Before leaving, she pulled me close to her on the bed, her hair now almost as white as the pillow. "Jesus is looking out for me," she said softly. "Remember me tonight when you say your prayers."

I did. I prayed that she would come home soon from the hospital.

But she didn't. I was not told she had inoperable cancer of the stomach. Mother avoided talking about her condition at all. Finally one night I angrily confronted my mother as she sat before her makeup mirror.

"You keep lying to me about Grandmother. Why doesn't she come home?"

Mother wheeled about, face flushed. "Your grandmother has cancer and is going to die. You just better face up to it."

"I don't believe you," I cried. "It isn't true!" Mother had lied to me before and I tried to convince myself that she was lying again.

That night I prayed that God would let my grandmother live.

Two days later she died. I was crushed, betrayed again. There was just no one you could trust.

I was home when Mother came back from the hospital. As she walked in the front door carrying Grandmother's small brown suitcase, I began to sob. This was all that was left of her. With sudden rage, I grabbed the suitcase out of my startled mother's hands and ran upstairs with it to my room.

Locking the door behind me, I threw the case on top of my bed. For a long time I lay there with my arms wrapped around the unopened suitcase, pouring out all my pent-up grief in wracking sobs. Then I opened the suitcase and carefully unpacked it: a bathrobe, nightgown, slippers, comb, brush, toothbrush, toothpaste, pictures of my mother and me and a pale blue ribbon which she wore in her hair. I put each item carefully in my drawer. They were mine now and no one could touch them.

The next day we went to the funeral home to see Grandmother lying in her casket. I was shocked. This shrunken thing in the casket didn't look at all like my grandmother. What had they done to her in the hospital?

For a long time I stood there, staring. Then I moved over to the casket, reached in and touched Grandmother's hands. They were stiff and cold.

From my pocket I pulled out half of Grandmother's blue hair ribbon. The other half of it was back in my drawer. I didn't know where to put it so I laid it on the pillow beside her white hair.

My desolation was total. The only person I felt ever really loved me was dead. And now everything she represented was gone. Her God was a fraud or else He would have answered my prayers. Life was a cheat.

As I stood next to the casket, I felt completely alone. Was there anyone anywhere who could meet the aching need inside me for a deep and satisfying love?

3

Broadway

WITH MY GRANDMOTHER'S death, something seemed to die within me as well. Not faith, because I had never believed in a loving God. But what I loved had either died or rejected me. Perhaps it was my belief in man's goodness that expired. I concluded that if I were to succeed it would be through my own efforts. Since the world of make believe seemed the best road to fulfillment for me, I decided at 15 to leave both school and Florida and go to New York for a career in the theatre.

Mother consented to this only if my father would assume financial responsibility. By this time she had sold our house, found her own apartment and become a real estate agent. Dad agreed to help me and I enrolled in a ten-week acting course at the Bown-Adams Professional Studio in New York. There I made an important discovery: I had talent. I was a chameleon in my ability to assume different roles. My mind was a blotter in its knack of absorbing details and dialogue.

Summer stock, I was told upon graduation from Bown-Adams, was the place to launch a career and acquire experience quickly. But I had no credits and no prospects of gaining any. As I wandered disconsolately down Broadway, an idea came to me. *Life With Father* was a long-run hit and the child actors in it had been changed repeatedly through the years. Since I was sure no summer stock producer could have kept up with the changes, I presented myself as a former member of the cast of *Life With Father*.

This got me a job with the Hawthorne Inn Playhouse in East Gloucester, Massachusetts, where I made my debut in the starring role of teen-aged Henry Aldrich in *What A Life*. More reward than my $45 weekly salary was savoring the sight of theatre posters emblazoned with my name in star billing above all the other actors.

To gain more experience during 1947 and 1948, I performed winter stock roles at the Princess Hotel on Daytona Beach and summer stock at Tuxedo, North Carolina and Mt. Gretna, Pennsylvania. Then in the summer of 1948, when I was 18, I played young Marchbanks in George Bernard Shaw's *Candida* with the Williamsport Stock Company in Pennsylvania.

Sure enough, the stage filled that yawning hole inside me and I felt alive only when I was before the footlights playing someone else. When the lights went out at the end of a show, it was almost as if my soul had been extinguished at the same time. When I wiped makeup off my face, it was as if I was removing the real Jay Robinson, leaving someone else nakedly revealed. To be whole I needed the spotlight on me; applause became my substitute for love.

After several years in a dozen such productions, I decided it was time to make my real assault on Broadway. But Broadway, run by hard-eyed businessmen, seemed an unclimbable mountain for a teen-ager. So I had to be audacious. While my summer stock roles had given me stage presence and developed my acting skills, I lacked the credits that would get me past the secretary of any Broadway producer. Unless I used every bit of brass and guile I possessed.

Then came an idea. The lie about my acting experience in *Life With Father* had gotten me into summer stock. Why not stretch it and fabricate some credits in the British theatre? I could certainly put on the proper British accent.

The English theatre, much admired by American professionals, was too far away for easy checking. I would be an American, educated in England, who had extensive experience there in repertory theatre.

But first I had to have an agent. I'd heard about Olga Lee who was one of the smaller agents but had a prestigious client list. I made an appointment. Dressed in my best jacket and assuming what I thought was a London swagger, I sauntered into Miss Lee's office.

She nearly floored me with her first question. "If you are an American, young man, how were you permitted to work there in the English theatre?"

Inwardly I fumbled desperately for an answer. Suddenly it came. "I have dual citizenship," I replied as calmly as my close brush with early disaster would permit. I must have carried it off for she accepted this and seemed impressed by my false credits and experience.

Weeks later I was visiting my mother in Miami Beach when the telegram came.

> *Will you fly to New York with no commitment on either side to read for part in "The Shop at Sly Corner" with Boris Karloff?*
>
> *Olga Lee*

Not even bothering to pack the right clothes, I took the first available flight and arrived at LaGuardia in a snowstorm. Though shivering without an overcoat, birds sang in my ears and my heart pounded with joy. I could already see my name up in lights on Broadway.

In the morning, with jacket collar turned up for warmth, I walked into Producer Gant Gaither's office with the assumed aplomb of a sophisticated Londoner, hiding a wildly beating heart. *The Shop at Sly Corner*, an English play, was to be directed by Margaret Perry, daughter of Antoinette Perry after whom the Tony Awards were named. The role for which I was to try out was that of Archie Fellowes, a despicable young cockney clerk who became a blackmailer.

Until that moment I had never tried out for a villainous part; all my roles had been healthy juvenile leads. But as I began to read lines from the script, I found it easy to slip into the role of this evil man, helped by my teen-aged masquerade as a cockney lad years before in Miami Beach.

The venom in my soul came out in that cockney accent. I willed myself to feel snide and vicious. The assemblage in the office seemed impressed but made no commitment.

I went back to my room and tried to relax. At four o'clock that afternoon, Olga Lee phoned with the good news. I was offered the role. I immediately sent a wire to my mother:

Have just signed run of play contract at $300 weekly to play leading role in "The Shop at Sly Corner." Am terribly happy and too excited to write.

Jay

The telegram contained two bold-faced lies. My salary was one third of that amount and it was not really a run-of-the-play contract. In reality I was on probation with a five-day escape clause at the producer's discretion. If I didn't deliver, I could be unloaded like a sack of rotten potatoes. But I had to act the role of a successful actor, even with Mother.

When we started rehearsing December 1, I found myself face to face with the master monster himself, the Frankenstein of actors, Boris Karloff. Still a teen-ager, I felt tremendous awe to be playing a leading role on Broadway with a star of his stature.

His real name was William Henry Pratt and he had been a schoolmaster in his native England. A kind and gentle man, he was considerate of everyone at all times. But as the rehearsals began, I became more and more self-conscious of my phoney British accent in front of a native Englishman. The five-day escape clause in my contract became a growing torment as the days of rehearsal passed. Would they keep me on?

The trial period was over. I had made it. I was thrilled when I read my glowing biography in the playbill. "Although American born, Mr. Robinson was educated in England and is thus comparatively new to the American scene. He has appeared in many plays in England, including *Candida, Ghosts, Young Woodley, Come of Age, Fata Morgana,* and *Night Must Fall.* He has many friends on both sides of the Atlantic who are watching his theatrical progress with interest."

I couldn't help smile at this last line; I had never once been outside the continental United States.

With rehearsals completed we went on the road for tryouts. This was a standard shakedown procedure to polish the production before facing the eagle eyes of the New York critics. Since their reviews. could kill a show, it was worth the extra expense.

We opened in Boston on Christmas night 1948 for a two-week run at the old Wilbur Theatre. The high point of the play was in the second act when Karloff throttled me for my despicable acts. He had huge hands and the awesome memory of him as a monster had lurked in my mind ever since I had seen *Frankenstein*. Each time we played the throttling scene, the same thing happened to me. The moment I felt his giant hands around my neck, my imagination took over and his face became that of Frankenstein's monster. I could even see the bolts in his neck. I never had to act in that scene. I was so frightened at that moment that my fear could be felt by the audience; the atmosphere in the theatre was electric.

Our notices were good and the Boston critics said that I had "stolen the show." Karloff, far from being jealous, insisted that I be awarded my own curtain call at the play's end. I did not try to understand or appreciate his thoughtfulness. Instead, I was overwhelmed by the waves of applause that surged over me from the darkness beyond the footlights' glare. It was like some warm, live thing pawing and caressing my ego.

If the world loved me as a villain, then a villain I would be!

From Boston we moved on to Philadelphia where our notices were equally as good. Once again I was singled out for special praise. The heavy applause convinced me even more that we had a hit on our hands and that my career was made. Now for Broadway!

We opened in the Booth Theatre right on Shubert Alley, the shrine of the American theatre. Though elegant, wealthy, and super sophisticated, the first nighters made a cold audience, guarding their applause like the Tower of London's Beefeaters protect the Crown Jewels. Every reaction had to be pried from them like taking a pearl from an oyster.

It is a custom to hold an after-the-show party at Sardi's, with Vincent Sardi himself at the door to welcome everyone. With the meal completed, we waited to read the reviews. At around 1 A.M. the first editions of the *Times* and the *Herald Tribune* arrived. There

were nine papers in New York then, but these were the most powerful.

Shouts rang out as hands excitedly turned the pages. Then came
a hush. The reviews gave our play faint praise, saying it was "just
another British play that did not travel well across the Atlantic."

But I had been singled out for an extraordinary performance:

New York Times: Horribly plausible. Sleek and stealthy and contempti-
ble.

New York Herald Tribune: An acid portrayal . . . splendid job.

New York News: Jay Robinson does a capital job as the little stinker
. . . he has a great deal of the quality that a young Emlyn Williams
showed in "Night Must Fall."

Show Business: Robinson wrapped up the show and walked away with
it . . . brilliant.

When I returned to the theatre for the second night's performance,
the notice announcing our closing that Saturday was already on
the stage door bulletin board. I was thunderstruck. My first leading
role on Broadway was in a flop and lasted only seven performances.
I had not realized that weak reviews killed a play. I had thought
it would run for years.

Boris Karloff took it like the seasoned trouper he was and signed
a photo for me with the inscription: "Dear Jay: I can truthfully
say that in all my long career in crime, you are the best victim I
ever throttled. Good luck: Boris."

Producer Gant Gaither, impressed by my performance and favorable notices, began looking around for a play in which he could
star me. The William Morris Agency now gave me the royal treatment to lure me away from Olga Lee. It was flattering to be courted
by the biggest agency in the business. But with big agencies, this
is standard operating procedure. And, as with many other young
actors, I yielded to their flattery and left Olga Lee.

Gaither acquired a play titled, *Gayden,* featuring a psychopathic, sinister young man in the lead role. He offered me the lead at $500 a week, and acquired Fay Bainter to play my mother. Miss Bainter had won an Academy Award some years earlier for best supporting actress as Bette Davis' mother in *Jezebel,* and here I was still a teenager playing opposite her. At 19 I was the youngest star on Broadway. In one season I had two major roles. I was ecstatic.

My success called for a more elegant address. Under pressure from his demanding son, Dad agreed to pick up the $400 monthly tab and I moved into a suite at the celebrity-haunted Algonquin Hotel where I could rub shoulders with America's famous men and women of letters. I became a first nighter, strolling down the theatre aisle in a tux with a white silk scarf tossed casually around my neck, a la Barrymore. I would turn my profile left and right, head slightly elevated, also in the Barrymore manner. My final touch was a scarlet silk-lined opera cloak draped over my shoulders.

Once again, the reviews killed *Gayden* but singled me out for praise.

Cue Magazine: Brilliantly venomous . . . superbly despicable.

New York Post: The play belongs to Mr. Robinson in the title role.

Wall St. Journal: An outstanding performance. I found him thoroughly monstrous and charming.

Show Business: One of the most fascinating performances I have ever seen.

Two flops in one season didn't discourage me and when Katharine Hepburn was lured back to Broadway by the Theatre Guild to star in Shakespeare's *As You Like It,* I was eager to audition for a role in the play. Usually, at the end of an audition, a voice floats across the footlights in a most disconcerting manner. The director thanks you and says they will let you know.

But this audition was different. As soon as I finished my reading, a lithe form in a slack suit literally bounded across the footlights.

It was Miss Hepburn, and with that rich throaty voice she said almost passionately, "Thank you, Mr. Robinson, that was wonderful. Will you join our company?"

We opened at the Cort Theatre on Broadway in January 1950 and played for five months. During this time I learned how considerate Kate could be. At one point I acquired a bad cold. Every day she brought me hot soup in my dressing room.

Katharine Hepburn was strong in other ways. She detested dirt and would thoroughly clean her dressing room. If she saw dirt anywhere else backstage, she'd take a broom and clean it up herself. She jogged several miles each day in Central Park, her chauffeured limousine following slowly.

According to backstage talk, Spencer Tracy came to the theatre most evenings to see the love of his life perform. But not one member of the cast ever saw him, although we all strained our eyes in the attempt.

Kate's brother, Richard, was not only our assistant stage manager but also my understudy. The theatre is full of stories about how understudies try to undermine the actors whose part they want to play. Not so with Richard.

He and Kate invited me for a weekend of skiing in Connecticut. Being a Florida kid, I had never been on skis. I started down a beginner's slope, wobbling erratically and staying upright only by leaning on the athletic Kate.

Suddenly I hit a rock, fell and injured my neck. Groaning with pain, I was rushed back to New York where my neck was put in traction using a cumbersome contraption of ropes, pulleys and weights. I was still in traction on Monday when Kate phoned, imploring me to get up and come to the theatre.

"I can't, Kate. I'm in too much pain," I said.

"You must, Jay," she replied. "Dick's petrified and refuses to go on in your place. You must come," she said, desperation creeping into her voice, "or the performance will be cancelled."

I was taken out of traction, and Kate sent her limousine to rush me to the theatre where I performed in considerable pain.

Concern for my billing in the play nearly did me in. It was somewhat less than my previous two shows. So I put another of my

bright ideas into action. I phoned all the New York papers, telling
them I was the Theatre Guild's press agent, and said, "Please move
Jay Robinson up to equal billing with Katharine Hepburn in your
listing. He has had a change of contract."

And that's what every paper in New York did, until the Theatre
Guild noticed it and changed it back again.

But while sharing equal billing with Kate, I was terrified that
my duplicity would be found out. One day Karl Nielsen, the stage
manager at the Cort Theatre, called me. Certain that my ploy had
been discovered and I was about to be fired, I avoided his call.
Although I had had little contact with my father during this period,
I turned to him now in desperation, calling him at his office at
the Van Heusen Company for advice. He told me to face up to
the situation and admit what I had done.

Reluctantly I returned Nielsen's call, my heart pounding. He
only had a routine question; the call had been blown out of propor-
tion by my guilty conscience. Once more I had gotten away with
deception.

Not content with starring on Broadway, I now proposed to become its youngest producer. The play *The Green Bay Tree* appealed
to me, mostly because it had a wonderful part I wanted to play.
I talked my father into raising $50,000 from business associates
to produce the play. When I was strongly advised that starring in
a play, plus producing it, would be too much for one person, I
hired Shepard Traube as producer-director.

Though I was to receive $500 a week as its young star, plus
fifty percent of any profits, I was persuaded to give control of casting
to Shepard Traube. For the other starring role he hired Joseph
Schildkraut, a brilliant but egocentric actor. My youthful arrogance
hit a raw nerve in Schildkraut and he began verbally assaulting
me every day. Finally he went to Traube and demanded that I be
replaced. Since Traube was fed up with my egotism too, he agreed.
So I was summarily fired. As a final blow, I heard Traube say in
a very loud voice as I staggered out of the theatre in sick fury,
"Get his name off the marquee—*now!*"

Wild with anger, ill with embarrassment and humiliation, I
stormed out of New York to Miami Beach to nurse my wounds

in my mother's hotel apartment to which she had moved after Grandmother's death. The weeks in southern Florida were spent fuming and raging. Seeing that I was near a breakdown, Mother got a doctor for me. My despair continued, not at all assuaged when *The Green Bay Tree* folded after a short Broadway run.

Healing of a sort came when I met the Australian writer, Sumner Locke Elliott. When I told him my tale of woe, to my amazement he broke up in near-hysterical laughter, declaring it was the funniest story he had ever heard. "Therein lies a play," he said and asked for my permission to write it. Eagerly I gave it, believing the play would be a big hit. The title: *Buy Me Blue Ribbons.*

To produce it, I went back to my father, pressing him for the financing. He came through with another $50,000 but at a sacrifice I didn't learn about until years later. Cyril Ritchard was persuaded to come from Australia to direct. But, having been burned once, this time I retained total control of the production.

I rented the Empire Theatre, one of Manhattan's most beautiful, primarily because it was in the same building as Shepard Traube's office. So he could not fail to get the message, I put my name up in lights ten feet high. I knew that Joseph Schildkraut went in and out of Traube's office regularly.

Really it was a ridiculous situation. I owned the play, was my own producer and star in a story based on my own life. Yet I was still a kid of only 21. My primary goal was to regain my stature and show up my two enemies. The play opened on Broadway before a stiff audience and an inscrutable row of reviewers. Afterwards we all repaired to Sardi's where I had arranged a luxurious dinner party with champagne. There we awaited the reviews.

They were brought to me by the last person I expected to see. I can still recall him slowly marching up the stairs at Sardi's, arms loaded with newspapers, a smug smile on his face. Joseph Schildkraut had brought them personally.

Handing them to me, he said in his accented English, "I knew you would want to have these."

The critics were merciless. Two reviews have become classics:

Walter Kerr wrote in the *Herald-Tribune:* "Mr. Robinson is suffering from delusions of adequacy."

The other: "If Mr. Robinson is not careful, he will go down to posterior."

I was destroyed.

I managed to do one more play on Broadway, Shakespeare's *Much Ado About Nothing,* in May of 1952, but the results were anything but encouraging. The despondency of that personal failure was too overwhelming for anything to be of comfort.

It was January 20, 1953. As I fled through the airport lobby on my way to Florida and to Mama, they were selling special editions of newspapers with giant banner heads: "IKE AND DICK INAUGURATED."

I remember thinking, "I should have gone into politics. Nothing as bad as what had happened to me could ever happen to Eisenhower or Nixon."

4

Two Life-Changing Words

THE ROAD TO MY strange destiny in Hollywood took some odd twists and turns during the next months. Wounded deeply by my Broadway failures, I decided on a vacation trip to a series of exotic places. In need of a father figure on whom I could lean when my inner distress mounted, I asked my friend Leo Riley to join me. Leo was a New York writer whose ferocious appearance and tremendous bulk made him look like a Sumo wrestler. Inside he was softhearted and gentle. Together we began our trip by flying to Havana, Cuba—a wide-open vacation spot in its pre-Castro days.

On our first evening in Havana, we headed for one of the seamier sections where we were beset by a horde of "guides" offering every vice and perversion imaginable.

"Don't get in any of their cars," counselled Leo, who was more worldly than I. My only exposure to life at that point had been on the stage. I did not drink or smoke, but I was both naive and adventurous—always a dangerous combination. Disregarding Leo's advice I accepted the offer of the most respectable-looking guide and climbed into his car, hoping for some excitement. Reluctantly, Leo climbed in too.

We drove for miles through the darkened streets of the city, finally stopping in front of a two-story house with dark green shutters covering the windows. Over the door, suspended on a wire, was a naked red bulb. It was one of Havana's famous bordellos.

The door was opened by a very fat woman in a cotton Mother Hubbard type dress hanging loosely on her immense frame. Quickly sizing up the two Americans, she motioned us inside. I eagerly followed her, but Leo refused to enter the place, mounting guard outside instead.

I was guided upstairs and into a room occupied by two scantily dressed girls and three native men. They were circulating one ragged-looking, strange-smelling cigarette, each taking a couple of deep puffs before passing it on again.

When it was offered to me, I declined. "I don't smoke," I said in English. This got a laugh and the cigarette was then given to someone else.

I sat down in a nearby chair and studied the scene. There was a wildness in their faces that was frightening. Suddenly a half dozen men seemed to materialize out of the woodwork. They stood around me in a silent but threatening circle. I was dragged roughly to my feet, slapped up against the wall; two men held me there while the others searched my clothes. Fortunately for me I put up no resistance. Shortly afterwards, I was lucky enough to find myself out on the street, unharmed, but minus all my cash, my watch and both our return airline tickets. Leo met me shaking his head.

Between us, we did not have even the price of a taxi back to our hotel and had no idea where we were. But Leo, with an unerring sense of direction, led me, footsore and aching, into our room just as dawn was breaking.

How were we going to get back home? Luckily Leo had a large gold ring given him by his mother. We pawned it at an Havana hockshop. We did not get enough money to buy tickets to Miami, so settled for Key West, the nearest point to Cuba. Our Cuban adventure had lasted one day.

In Key West we checked into a second-rate rooming house and I wired my father for money.

Our next destination was New Orleans and Mardi Gras. We decided to rent costumes and I eagerly explored the roles I might play during the carnival debauchery. Napoleon Bonaparte was a possibility. What fun to be this arrogant hero whom the world admired! But the costume fit poorly. The hunchback of Notre Dame was another possibility. But this didn't work out either so I settled for a French apache dancer, hardly aware of the instinctive way I sought to play offbeat characters.

When Mardi Gras was over, Leo and I headed for Mexico City. It was time again for another telegram to Dad. My father's attitude toward my continuous requests for money was predictable. He would caution me softly about my impetuousness, warn me about extravagance, but always come through if I seemed desperate enough. I soon learned how to make my condition appear critical.

For our trip to Mexico City we took a battered rural bus complete with chickens and a multitude of passengers. On the long journey I came down with "Montezuma's Revenge" and was shaken with terrible cramps and stomach pains. At frequent intervals I was forced to stop the bus to avoid embarrassing myself. It became quite comical for my Mexican fellow travelers. The thin, pale gringo kept getting off the bus miles from anywhere and dashing behind the nearest sheltering shrubbery or rocks, only to stagger back to the bus a few minutes later even more pale, much weaker and perspiring profusely. At this point all the Mexican passengers would shower me with a lively chorus of "Ole!"

From Mexico City we traveled to the then relatively unspoiled resort of Acapulco. Three businessmen we met on the beach offered us a ride back to the states. No matter how hot it was, these new acquaintances wore dark suits and hats throughout the long drive. They took turns at the wheel, driving some two thousand miles virtually nonstop to the border. Their sleek, black car seemed a block long. The language was rough, the stories they told crude; yet having become accustomed to such accents and jargon in New York I hardly noticed. When an automatic pistol worn in a shoulder holster was unveiled by a carelessly unbuttoned jacket, I became nervous. The men were racketeers. Were Leo and I in for more trouble?

In Juarez, our "friends" dropped us off at a motel and said they would pick us up the next morning for the drive to Los Angeles. To our great relief they never showed up.

It was time for my father again! He could certainly keep track of our progress by the urgent telegrams.

Leo and I arrived by bus in Los Angeles on March 12, 1953, checking into the Biltmore Hotel. We were so dirty and rumpled I'm surprised they gave us a room. I had no way of knowing that in the next nine days my whole life was to undergo a tremendous change.

On March 21, the day before we were to return to New York City, I looked through the yellow pages of the Los Angeles area for any listing of theatrical agents who were associated with east coast offices. My thought was to line up a part in a play.

Paul Small was listed; I knew him by reputation—a former vaudevillian turned agent. On an impulse I called and asked for Paul but instead was referred to one of his associates, an Englishman named Peter Shaw. I introduced myself as a New York actor.

"What parts have you played on Broadway?" asked Peter.

"I've been a blackmailer, a fop and a psychopathic murderer," I answered.

"Hmm. Interesting," he said. "Stay at that number and I'll call you back."

The phone rang again an hour later. "You may be in luck," he began. "Twentieth Century Fox is making *The Robe,* based on the book by Lloyd C. Douglas. It'll be one of the biggest pictures in the history of Hollywood. They're pouring millions into it to introduce the new Cinemascope process. Richard Burton, Jean Simmons and Victor Mature are the stars."

I was impressed. "Do you see something in this for me?"

"Possibly. One of the most coveted parts is that of the mad Roman Emperor Caligula. Based on your Broadway experience, this might be a part for you. They're looking for the curious combination of a young actor who can play an evil role."

In spite of my condescending attitude toward films, I became eager for the part.

"I'll phone you if there's any interest," said Shaw.

I didn't have long to wait. He called me back almost immediately to say he had arranged a meeting with Billy Gordon, Fox's casting director. "Would you come right over to my office?" he asked.

As he drove me over to the Fox lot in his convertible, Peter Shaw filled me in on this interesting part. It seemed that after an exhaustive series of tests for the role of Caligula, Twentieth Century Fox had settled on a brilliant young actor named John Buckmaster, son of the esteemed British actress, Gladys Cooper. John had gotten the attention of theatrical people while appearing in a George Bernard Shaw play in New York. One night he suddenly dashed out of his apartment into the street nude. He was arrested but later released so he could finish his role in the play. Fox chose to ignore this warning signal.

Now they were a third of the way into the movie, the Caligula costumes had already been made to Buckmaster's measurements, and they were about to shoot the Caligula scenes. Suddenly Buckmaster had another breakdown; he was taken from the stage directly to a sanitarium and was not expected to be released for a long time.

There is a strange connecting anecdote to this story. John Buckmaster was a close friend of Vivien Leigh who at this time had a breakdown of her own and was removed from her starring role in *Elephant Walk,* to be replaced by Elizabeth Taylor. Vivien's husband, Laurence Olivier, rushed to America and flew her home to England on a stretcher. This had been worldwide news while Buckmaster's collapse went almost unnoticed.

The Fox executives were frantic. With their biggest film ever already in production, they had lost their Caligula. Peter Shaw then went on to give me a capsule story of this strange Roman emperor. Gaius Caesar Augustus Germanicus was one of nine children, the son of Germanicus Caesar and Agrippina, the granddaughter of Caesar Augustus. As a child Gaius acquired the name Caligula which means "Little Boots." It was given him by the soldiers when they saw him playing about his father's army camp in a soldier's uniform, complete with tiny military boots. When the Roman Emperor Tiberius died in A.D. 37, Caligula, then 25, ascended the throne.

At first he was a benevolent emperor and won popularity by, among other things, eliminating some of the taxes imposed by Tiberius. Then something strange happened to Caligula during an illness; after recovering, he became a wild, profligate dictator. His sexual actions became a scandal, his spending was a disaster, he conspired to murder military and political enemies, he imposed the death penalty indiscriminately. Then he decided that he was a god and would communicate audibly with Jupiter, conducting his conversations in temples he built for such pagan purposes. His cruelty became so extreme that he was finally assassinated at the age of 29.

"This could be our chance to make a terrific deal," Peter continued. "The studio needs a Caligula *now* and they're in a poor bargaining position. So act hard to get. You're a New York stage actor. Tell them that you are going back to New York to appear in a Broadway play and aren't really interested in the role."

"But I am," I protested.

"Well," replied Shaw, "the surest way of getting it is by making them think you are indifferent. If an actor is hungry, the price is cheap. If you play it my way, I think we can get a top price and a terrific contract."

He went on to tell me that if I got the role it would be for two movies to be shot back-to-back: *The Robe* and its sequel, *Demetrius and the Gladiators.*

We drove through the impressive entrance of Twentieth Century Fox's studios. I was taken into Gordon's office where I sat across from him, my legs crossed casually. Inside I was far from nonchalant.

Billy Gordon was a shrewd casting director and he studied me carefully from behind his desk. "How old are you?" he asked.

I was 22 but had been advised by Shaw to say I was 27 since Caligula had died at 29. "I'm 27," I lied.

"That's perfect," said Gordon with satisfaction.

While we talked, I instinctively found myself assuming the personality of Caligula. As my gestures became imperious and my voice authoritarian, I could see Gordon becoming more and more excited. He immediately took me over to the set to meet with Director Henry Koster and Producer Frank Ross. They were in the middle of a Richard Burton scene and I stood there enthralled as the magnificent Welshman delivered lines in his resonant, slightly nasal voice.

A test was set for two days later and I was given a script of the scene to study. It was a great part and I became so absorbed by the person of Caligula that I could hardly sleep.

I arrived well before the appointed time: 3 P.M. on March 23. I went through makeup, had my hair fixed properly, was arrayed in a toga by the wardrobe department and delivered to the stage. The test was to be directed by Delmer Daves who was already under contract to direct the "Demetrius" sequel.

Daves gave me some basic instructions and the set was lit for the scene. Before I knew what was happening, a disembodied voice said, "Action!" and for five minutes I *was* Caligula!

Then Delmer Daves called out, "Cut." To my surprise he added, "Print." Turning to me, he said, "Thank you, Mr. Robinson. That was magnificent."

Bewildered, I went back to the Biltmore to worry. Only one take? I felt I had not given a polished performance and in my tortured mind I thought I had muffed my chances despite the director's compliment.

My friend Leo Riley encouraged me to wait patiently for the result and flew on to New York by himself. I never saw Leo again. Two days passed and I began to feel that the studio would not even bother to call me. In the agony of uncertainty I began to pack my bag when the phone rang. It was Shaw. He was beside himself with excitement. Darryl Zanuck had seen the test at 3 A.M. that morning and sent a terse two-word memo to Billy Gordon: "Take him."

I was Caligula.

The deal was unbelievable. A two-month contract at $3,000 a week on *The Robe,* and an additional three months on *Demetrius and the Gladiators* at the same salary. Twentieth Century Fox was also taking a seven-year option on my future services.

My feet hardly touched the ground during the days that followed. I fervently believed that through the person of Caligula I would at last find the fulfillment for which I yearned.

5

Emperor of Hollywood

HOW STRANGE IS the Hollywood star system. Only a handful of men at Twentieth Century Fox had seen my test. Yet those two words—"take him"—by the head of the studio transformed my life. Part of it was the large salary. Part of it was the word-of-mouth grapevine that fed my insatiable ego. Part of it was the chemistry of the role which I soon embraced on and off the screen.

Telephone calls to my parents had predictable results. My father congratulated me quietly, Mother was jubilant. She had once rejected a Hollywood offer in favor of marriage and had regretted what she considered lost star opportunities ever since. She now took the first flight to Los Angeles to be with the son she had had so little contact with all his life.

We took a second floor apartment at the corner of Beverly Green and Pico Boulevard, only two blocks from the studio. This meant I could walk to work. The apartment beneath us was the residence of the eminent scholar-philosopher-author, Aldous Huxley. Mother was now able to boast, "I live over Aldous Huxley."

Mr. Huxley, I'm afraid, did not share our neighborly enthusiasm. I bought a monkey soon after moving into our new apartment and turned him loose. He would climb and scamper around the apartment all day and much of the night. Lamps, bric-a-brac, books and sundry articles were constantly set flying to thunder down upon the head of Aldous Huxley, hardly conducive to writing a learned

44

tome on some deep subject. Mr. Huxley beat a path to the manager's office so often with complaints about us, I was forced to cage "Little Boots," the name we chose for the monkey. Even a pet had to be named after Caligula.

I developed a close relationship with the Twentieth Century Fox publicity people. Publicists like Frank Neill, Jet Fore and Harry Brand, head of the department, went to great efforts on my behalf. Sonia Wofson wrote a sixteen page biography on me, one of the longest ever written in Hollywood. One spurious item I gave her was that I had been educated by a private tutor as a child. This didn't jibe too well with my earlier claim in Broadway playbills of education in England, but nobody noticed the slight change in vital statistics. I began to wonder. Could one say anything about his past and get away with it?

Charles LeMaire designed my Caligula wardrobe. This thrilled my mother since thirty years earlier he had designed stage costumes for her. The elegant crown of gold laurel he created for me had one distinctive feature: The two top laurel leaves were turned upward to create the effect of little horns sticking out from my head. Billy Gordon said later that when I had assumed the personality of Caligula during our first meeting, he could see those little horns in his mind's eye. How well my early fantasies and Broadway parts had prepared me for this satanic role!

The Caligula hairstyle created for me by the studio later became a cult fashion worn widely by high school kids and many others across the country. It was known as the "Caesar" haircut.

The Twentieth Century Fox publicity mills began to grind. Darryl Zanuck had ordered an all-out campaign on me. I was constantly amazed to see my photo staring out from the pages of magazines and newspapers. My name appeared almost daily in the columns. At first I didn't understand how it worked but later spent part of each day watching the publicists, listening to their phone calls to editors pushing Jay Robinson to the press.

When we started shooting the Caligula scenes, I acted my heart out, playing to other players and the crew as if they were a Broadway audience. I felt a tremendous affinity for the part. Perhaps it stemmed from the poison and anger bottled up inside me from so many childhood frustrations and hurts. A more likely reason was the way it fed my never-satisfied ego which always needed praise. I wanted to drink more and more of the bubbling wine of fame and success.

At the end of a take on the first day, the whole film crew erupted in applause. Costar Jean Simmons turned to me and said: "I don't know if you are aware how rarely that happens." It was to happen eleven times during production.

Word began to circulate through the studio grapevine that something unusual was happening on our set and we began to get many visitors including such stars as Marilyn Monroe, Clark Gable, Gary Cooper and Humphrey Bogart.

The anamorphic Cinemascope lens was so new that no one really knew its demands. To make sure, the studio used much hotter lighting than usual and I sweated profusely beneath my armor. Neither heat nor long hours on my feet diminished the intensity of my work.

At one point I was in a long shot. The camera was far away getting panoramic atmosphere. I emoted as if the camera was recording every twitch on my face. The assistant director came up to me and said, "Don't work so hard, Jay. They can't even see you." On one silent shot, I orated with intense passion and full voice. I was always on stage and loved every minute of it.

Soon I was put on the "A" list of stars and moved to a magnificent dressing room suite. For lunch I was ushered to the area of the commissary where only the top stars were seated. More and more I was becoming a real-life Caligula.

Our final scene in *The Robe* was the trial. In my massive reception hall I sit on my throne triumphantly as a line of trumpeters in imperial colors stand motionless. The echoing chamber is crowded with the elite of Rome: senators, tribunes, officers and their ladies. Also stationed in strategic locations are members of my Praetorian Guard. Jean Simmons as Diana stands among them.

I set the stage for the trial to come. "Senators, Tribunes, Romans. We have been moved by your many expressions of loyalty to your Emperor. Our mission, as you all know, our divine mission is to further the welfare of the Empire."

Pausing for effect, I sit forward on my throne. "Is there anyone here who does not support us in this?"

A roar of loyalty fills the great hall: "NO!"

"And what must the Emperor decree for those who betray the Empire?"

The response is deafening: "Death . . . Death . . . Death!"

I sit back on my throne, smug and secure.

"You have spoken. As you know there exists today in our Empire, and even in Rome itself, a secret party of seditionists who call themselves 'Christians.' " I spit the word at them. I paint a picture of their disloyalty and rebellion and then come to the one point I want to make. "But now it grieves us to inform you that one of our own tribunes has betrayed his trust and joined this party of conspirators."

Shocked cries.

"Bring in Tribune Marcellus Gallio."

The trumpets blare, drums roll and, surrounded by a tight guard, Richard Burton as Marcellus enters carrying the robe in a pouch under his arm.

I challenge him. "Tribune Gallio, you have been informed of the charges against you?"

"I have, Sire."

"You stand before the senators and tribunes of Rome. They wait to hear your defense."

Marcellus looks around at the gathering of his peers and friends. "It's true that I am a Christian." A gasp rushes from the entire hall. When the hubbub subsides, Marcellus continues. "It's not true that those of us who try to follow the teachings of Jesus are engaged in any plot against the state."

"But isn't it a fact that you call this Jesus a king?" I purr.

"Yes, Sire."

"Ha!"

"But His kingdom is not of this world. He seeks no earthly throne. He reigns over the hearts and minds of men, in the name of justice and charity."

"And are these virtues not to be found in our Empire?" I ask.

Marcellus replies in a voice so quiet, all have to strain their ears to hear the reply. "Was it justice, or was it charity that gave me my orders when I put Him to death on a cross?"

I am astounded to hear these words. "*YOU* put Him to death? Then why are you risking your life to serve as His ambassador?"

"I owe Him more than my life. He forgave me my crime against Him."

The trial moves on. "What's that thing you're holding?" I finally ask.

"His robe. He wore it to the cross."

My voice is tense. "Let me see it."

Marcellus holds the pouch out before him and I reach for it—but suddenly push it away. "No," I cry, "it's bewitched." I quickly regain my composure and turn back to Marcellus.

"Tell me, Tribune, do you expect us to believe these stories that this Jesus could heal by the touch of His hand, make the crippled walk and the blind see again?"

Marcellus puts up a spirited defense of his fake king, Jesus, but he is preaching to deaf ears.

"You have heard him," I snarl to the assembly. "He stands convicted out of his own mouth. What is your pleasure?"

The crowd is quiet, but my faithful Quintus, who has worked his way down into the crowd, raises a clenched fist and shouts in a voice to fill the hall and send the echoes reverberating. "DEATH!"

Some of the crowd take up the cry. To my rage I see many who stand silent. I mark them in my mind for future attention.

Now I change my strategy. "Marcellus Gallio, kneel to us and renew your oath of loyalty to your Emperor. Renounce your misguided allegiance to this dead Jew who dared to call Himself a king."

The hall falls silent.

Marcellus drops to his knees and renews the pledge of loyalty as I had commanded.

"And the other—Jesus—renounce Him! So all can hear!" I shout gleefully.

"I cannot renounce Him, Sire. Nor can you. He is my King, and yours as well. He is the Son of God." He rises to his feet.

At this point Diana joins him. For a moment I am at a loss

for words. Then anger fills me. "The sentence is death," I shout. The hall is filled with a terrible silence.

As Diana and Marcellus are taken out, I am still shaking with rage. Even fear of death does not prevent these troublemakers from renouncing me, their Emperor, their true god, in favor of this dead Jew named Jesus.

With the shooting completed on *The Robe,* we got a three-week break before beginning production on "Demetrius" in which Victor Mature and Susan Hayward starred. Movie sequels are often disasters and Fox was careful never to use the word, although they wanted to cash in on *The Robe's* popularity.

As for me, I was riding the crest of a huge tidal wave of attention and had never been happier. Money was piling up in the bank. Everywhere I turned people paid attention to me. My twenty-third birthday had been celebrated on the set. A huge iced cake was borne in by Praetorian Guards, with twenty-three candles flaming and the entire cast and crew applauding. I no longer worried that I had lied about my age to Billy Gordon.

One day I was ushered out to the back lot to see my coliseum. The set builders had done their work well. As I stood surveying what appeared to be a massive granite structure of towering tiers, I again slipped into my role as the Roman Emperor. Pride filled my breast and nothing in the world seemed more magnificent. If I had examined it more carefully, I would have found that the coliseum was only a papier-mache and plaster facade built with the cheapest lumber.

I was working so hard I would literally collapse at the end of a day. The shooting over until the next morning, I would walk wearily the two blocks home, soak under a hot shower and, exhausted, climb into bed. My mother would then serve me a big steak with a baked potato.

My part in "Demetrius" was beefed up as a result of my acting in *The Robe.* I was in a great many scenes. We shot the final climax of *Demetrius and the Gladiators* in the boiling sun of a California August day. Victor Mature as Demetrius was flat on his back on

the coliseum sand waiting for my signal that would determine
whether his life would be taken or spared.

I am inflamed against Demetrius and his Christianity, however,
and my down-turned thumb signals his end. The Praetorian Guard
and the Roman audience would not have it. Demetrius is the darling
of the arena. My aide whispers in my ear. "Let him live, Sire.
They demand it."

"Demand it?" I scream. "No one makes demands of God." And
so I condemn Demetrius. I, Caligula, am God and my will is to
be done."

But the guards revolt. One giant in the arena leans back and
hurls a nine-foot long spear at me which pierces my chest, pinning
me to the throne. Caligula dies with all Rome looking on.

To obtain the maximum of realism, the spear was made in three
overlapping sections that telescoped on impact, giving the effect
of entering my body. I wore a molded steel plate against my flesh
with a three-inch-thick layer of cork between it and my toga.

The spear would travel on a wire which led to my chest. The
huge guard, whose biceps were immense, would throw the spear
with all his strength. It was supposed to travel up the wire like a
projectile, passing through the armor, with the cork taking most
of the shock, and stopping when it reached the steel plate I wore.

To heighten the drama of my death, I was actually standing at
my throne in suspension from four ropes. Two ropes from behind
the throne were fastened to my back, while two others from the
front of me were concealed by the rail before the throne. One man
was exerting pressure on each rope and I was held upright like
the pole of a tent.

When the spear hit me, the men in front were to let go, while
the two behind would pull on their ropes to yank me backwards
onto the throne itself.

Victor Mature was aghast. "Are you crazy, Jay?" he asked.
"Don't let them throw that thing at you. If the wire breaks you
could be blinded or killed. Use a double!"

But I ignored his advice. The scene had to be believable. Moreover,
I didn't want to give up one second of being before the camera.

Still, I was nervous. The joking of the cast and crew did not help. "Don't worry, Jay," one of them said. "That spear thrower has a tremendous arm. He rarely misses." Another added, "It's good they left this shot until the last. If you're killed, the picture is over anyway and it adds to the realism."

On the take, I stood suspended from the hidden ropes perspiring nervously.

The cameras rolled, the director shouted "Action!" and the spear thrower leaned back and in a paroxysm of strength hurled the long steel weapon at me. It streaked up the wire like a rocket, slamming into my chest with explosive force. Stunned by the blow despite the protection, I gasped as I was yanked backwards against the throne.

I finally managed to sit up, trying to catch my breath to hear the director say it had to be done all over again. By now I wished I had taken Victor Mature's advice.

Again and again I had to watch that giant spear scream up the wire at me. Finally, after the ninth take, the director was satisfied. I spent the evening in the bathtub recovering, with Mother hovering solicitously outside the door.

When production of "Demetrius" ended in August, it was time to prepare for the world premiere of *The Robe* at Grauman's Chinese Theatre on Hollywood Boulevard. A gold Cadillac convertible would carry me to the opening—just right for Caligula. The studio arranged for Anne Bancroft to be my date.

As my Cadillac neared the theatre, we passed by the bleachers which had been set up for blocks all along Hollywood Boulevard. They were packed with screaming fans. The pure white incandescent beams of the searchlights stabbed the sky. Banners were suspended between the street lamps over the boulevard. When Anne and I alighted in front of the theatre, we stepped onto acres of red carpeting.

Grauman's had been completely refurbished for *The Robe* and a huge crimson stage curtain curved in a graceful arc before the screen. Lit by strategically placed floodlights, it glowed like a huge bloodstain. Stereophonic sound was introduced to a theatre audience for the first time in this film and the audience was surrounded by sixteen speakers. They literally engulfed the audience in sound, and as the majestic "Robe" overture poured over me in waves, I felt the hair rising on the back of my neck.

The overture came to an end and as the lights dimmed, the curtain opened slowly. It was like the parting of the Red Sea. And then, there I was up on the screen, thirty feet high, and my fears ebbed.

The film came to its dramatic end, Richard Burton and Jean Simmons were led off to their execution. In their deaths, they and their Jesus had supposedly defeated me. There was a hush and then the theatre exploded with applause which went on and on. Great stars came over to where I was sitting to offer their congratulations.

As I groped up the aisle in a daze, hands reached to shake mine and voices came from out of a sea of faces to offer praise.

Caligula was not defeated, I thought. This is my triumph! I am still Emperor.

6

Star Treatment

ON SEPTEMBER 25, 1953, the day after the Chinese Theatre world premiere, ecstatic reviews of *The Robe* spread across the country. The queen of Hollywood gossip, Louella Parsons, said in her column, syndicated to more than a thousand papers worldwide: "The most spectacular premiere in the history of Hollywood. Jay Robinson makes his screen debut as Caligula and a more POISONOUS POR-TRAYAL you could never find . . . A great performance . . . A star is born."

Hedda Hopper agreed: "Stage, film offers *deluge* Jay Robinson, the sensation of the year in Hollywood."

How I lapped it all up. Across the country, the press reaction fell into the same pattern. *New Yorker* Magazine: "Unquestionably the most polished young actor of our times." *Time:* "Head and shoulders above his contemporaries." When I met President Dwight Eisenhower on the links of the Burning Tree golf course in Palm Springs, he praised my acting in *The Robe*. Any flicker of objectivity about myself was soon extinguished as the waves of praise rolled over me.

Opening day saw huge lines formed at the Chinese Theatre for every performance, stretching two full blocks on both sides of the theatre. As the days passed, the crowds grew larger. It became my favorite pastime to drive past the theatre several times a day checking the lines. There seemed to be no limit to my hunger for adulation.

Meanwhile Twentieth Century Fox kept me as an exclusive contract player on a large weekly salary and I sat back waiting for
my next role. At one point Louella Parsons, in her Hearst column,
said I was to replace Marlon Brando as Napoleon in *Desiree*.

The truth was that Marlon Brando was being truculent in his
demands and the studio was using my name to soften his stand.
Brando eventually played Napoleon.

Hedda Hopper had me cast as the Pharaoh Akenhaton in *The
Egyptian*. Wrong again. Michael Wilding got the "Egyptian" role.

But my fan mail kept me euphoric. The *Pittsburgh Press*:
"Caligula (Jay Robinson) surpasses Marilyn Monroe in fan mail."
The Boston Globe: "Robinson's fan mail rose to 10,300 letters during
a recent week." Fan clubs were started for me all over America.
The studio was delighted.

I took part in phony photo layouts "Jay Robinson cooking" (although I could not and never did cook); "Jay Robinson sailing";
" . . . at the beach." When I wasn't "doing" anything else I was
being interviewed. Every day produced a new series of clippings
about me.

Before the shooting was finished on "Demetrius" I had concluded
that my star status called for a big house and contacted a woman
realtor who read me perfectly. One day as we drove about, she
casually tossed into the conversation a baited hook which I snapped
at like a ravenous trout. "There's a house for sale in Bel Air on
Stone Canyon Road."

Bel Air was the *creme de la creme* of movie addresses. As we
drove about this area, she pointed out the homes of various stars.
I was in a daze of self-indulgence. The house for sale sat far back
from the road on a huge piece of land. It was all new, glittering
with what appeared to be acres of glass windows. And it was backed
by its own mountain.

The realtor was oh so casual. "You would," she said, "have to
landscape." She talked so artfully of tropical shrubbery and retaining
walls that I could actually see it all in place.

Inside the house I moved in a trance, drinking in the high-beamed
ceilings, the eighteen-foot fireplace and the entrancing waterfall in
the fifty-foot living room. The sunken Roman bath was fit only
for an emperor and the entire front of the house comprised sliding

glass panels, one hundred feet of them. I had found Caligula's palace in modern Babylon.

Before the agent had even finished her spiel, I had written a deposit check for $10,000. The house was mine. Soon the landscapers, builders and interior decorators took over. Several weeks later my mother and I moved in.

The gold carpet cost thousands of dollars, while a hundred feet of the most tantalizing drapery hung shielding the front windows. But my mother didn't stay long. She tried to temper my flights into a fantasy world and I rebelled. We quarreled frequently. When I told her it was my life and I would live it as *I* wished, she moved out, went back to her own apartment and began a career as a real estate broker in Santa Monica.

As *The Robe* sailed on for month after month of huge box office grosses, I sat like an emperor in my palace with nothing to do and the money rolling in each Friday. Warners wanted me for a star part in *The Silver Chalice,* but Fox refused permission on this and other offers. Thousands of fan letters a week were still pouring in as Caligula became the "cult" performance of the mid-1950s.

I started dating the boss' daughter, Susan Zanuck, and we were seen together frequently. She took me to the family beach house where I finally met her father. Then I gave Susan a monkey which escaped and wrecked her father's office. I'm sure this did nothing to advance my cause with him. Across the back of my house I had installed a large cage which was by now full of sundry simians.

I threw lavish parties in my Bel Air palace which were attended by top stars. Marilyn Monroe was a guest, as were Natalie Wood, Terry Moore, Mitzi Gaynor, Debbie Reynolds, Anne Francis, Jeff Hunter, Robert Wagner and Laurence Harvey.

Romanoff's catered these affairs and I would spend a thousand dollars or more on a huge buffet, spread upon snowwhite linen and adorned with the blazing color of fresh flowers. Caviar, Nova Scotia smoked salmon, prime rib roasts, capon in aspic, salads, desserts enticed the eye and satisfied the palate.

At one particular party, Mike Romanoff had done it again and the guests were lining up, plates in hand to enjoy the imperial repast.

However, a female gibbon ape slipped through the partially closed door of the cage behind the house. She glided into the dining room and scampered across the buffet, scattering plates and creating general panic. Upset by the shouting, the beast climbed upon a chandelier, and made a mess all over the food and my guests. The exodus that followed was as rapid and noisy as anything ever done on the "Keystone Kops."

Later, when my male gibbon, "Buster," escaped from the grounds, the press seized on the story with relish. The headlines blared: MAD EMPEROR'S APE LOOSE IN BEL AIR. Before the papers were through with it, the story sounded as if King Kong were on the loose with all Bel Air inhabitants locking their doors in panic. The next day two small girls, each holding one of "Buster's" hands, brought him back, scared and docile.

The animals served me in other ways too. I took to driving along Sunset Boulevard in my convertible, an ape sitting on each shoulder, helping me build an image of a real-life Caligula.

When *Demetrius and the Gladiators* premiered, I caught a curious change in Caligula on the screen from my seat in the darkened theatre. In a strange way he seemed to have become even more maniacal, almost as if that really wasn't me up there but someone else. I quickly dispelled the thought.

I kept so busy living the role of the mad Roman emperor and making personal appearances during the first two years of my stardom that there was little time for any other life. As the months passed without any new film role, each new day became more boring than the last.

The glitter of Hollywood had faded. I was sick of driving up Sunset Boulevard in my convertible and I began seeking out the company of a variety of unusual people.

One was a very wealthy and elderly woman, forty years my senior, who was eager to advance my career. In trying to look like a film siren, she had acquired black laquered hair and adorned her eyelids with sequins. I overlooked her bizzare affectations and let her take me to parties where I was quite willing to give private performances for the guests. She wrote to her friends in high Hollywood positions, urging them to find new starring roles for me.

I was in her home one night watching television in the living room when she called to me from her bedroom and said she had something to show me. Unsuspectingly I walked in. The woman lay in the middle of a large circular bed, leering at me from under her sequin-studded eyelids.

My shock was not what she had intended. While I stared at her unattractive form in dismay, her voice changed from a soft invitation to a rather strident demand. I turned and fled from the house, obscenities raining upon me.

Then there was the young woman who began writing me once a week after seeing *The Robe*. All of my fan mail was screened by studio secretaries who would handle picture requests and other routine inquiries. The more interesting letters would be sent on to me. Most I ignored, but this woman, whom I'll call Joan, caught my attention.

She was an eager student of Roman history and had a vast knowledge of Caligula. Each letter was filled with facts, dates and insights into the emperor's life. She saw *The Robe* over and over to study my characterization of Caligula. "I believe you are the reincarnated emperor," she wrote.

The letters were so interesting and well written, I found myself looking forward to receiving them. Then one arrived postmarked "Hollywood." "I am here in town," she wrote. "If you want to see me, call this number."

I stared at the telephone number for a long time, wondering what she was like. Something inside prodded me. I picked up the phone and dialed the number. A soft low voice answered.

"This is Caligula," I announced.

There was a gasp at the other end. Then silence for a few seconds. "May I see you?" she asked.

"Yes. Can you meet me in front of the Beverly Hills Hotel this afternoon at three o'clock?"

"I'll be there."

"How will I know you?"

"I'm young and have a Caesar haircut. I'll be wearing a red dress."

As three o'clock drew near, I began to question my impulsiveness. *She could be some kind of nut,* I thought. Then I reassured myself by saying that I could check her out, first by driving by the entrance. If she was impossible, I'd just drive away.

I backed my Cadillac convertible out of the garage, drove down Stone Canyon Road to Sunset Boulevard and turned left toward Beverly Hills. The hotel is set well back from the boulevard. Slowly I drove past the entrance. There in front stood a woman in a red dress. She had a Caesar haircut. She was in her twenties, slim and attractive. I stopped the car and beckoned her inside.

Joan sat down, closed the car door and stared at me for a long time before she spoke. "You really are Caligula," she finally said.

I asked her a question about the emperor's family. She responded with a long account of Caesar's life. Her voice was well modulated, her eyes were a startling gray-green. Her mind was sharp, knowledgeable. We drove around for a while and talked. Only one trait of hers made me uncomfortable—a certain flicker in her eyes when she looked at me.

"Would you like to see my home?" I asked.

"Yes."

We drove into the driveway, parked and I led her up the steps made from redwood rounds, past the banana plants, the great tree ferns and into the massive living room. With mouth open, she watched the waterfall foam onto a bed of rocks at the side of the room, stared at the huge stone fireplace. I took her out back, naming the tropical birds and plants, and introduced her to my collection of monkeys and apes in their giant cages.

"Sire, this is just what I expected," she said breathlessly. The obsequious greeting should have warned me. It didn't. Hours later I invited Joan to move in with me. And she did—that very evening.

Several weeks later we were sitting in front of the fireplace, talking again about the Roman empire. She told me how, as Caligula became bored with his pleasures, he went on to new excesses in cruelty and depravity. By now I was tired of her talk and a bit unnerved by the complete way Joan was living the role of Caligula's mistress. It was not just a fantasy with her; it was reality. I was Caligula. I was her emperor.

"Sire," she said suddenly. "I want to have your baby."

A spasm of fear shot down my backbone. "No, I don't want that," I said firmly.

Usually she accepted my commands. This time she did not. "My life will only have meaning if I can bear the child of Caligula." Her eyes flickered several times with a strange light, like fire about to break out in the green irises. Suddenly for me the affair was over.

Slowly I arose. "You are being disobedient. I am going out for a while. Don't wait up for me."

Her eyes flickered again, but she said nothing as I left the house. For hours I drove about wondering how to get Joan out of my life. It was well after midnight when I returned.

Softly I tiptoed to my room and opened the door. Joan was lying across my bed, asleep with her clothes on. I closed the door, slipped down the hall to the guest bedroom, undressed and was asleep within minutes.

I don't know what awoke me. But I looked up to see Joan standing over me, her face demonic, her right arm raised. The hall light glinted from a long thin blade clenched in her fingers.

"Drop that!" I gasped.

My voice startled her. Joan's arm slumped by her side and she looked at me guiltily.

"Why are you holding that knife?" My heart beat wildly.

"I don't know."

"Give it to me," I reached out a trembling hand.

She did so dutifully.

"Now go to your room and go to bed."

After seeing that Joan did as I ordered, I went to my own room, and locked the door. But there was no more sleep for me that night.

The next morning I knew exactly what to do. I confronted Joan as the enraged, betrayed emperor. She was to leave the house that day. She was to go home. When her things were packed, I called a cab.

There was no resistance, only complete submission. As she got in the cab, I gave her some money. She took it without thanks,

her face expressionless. Then there was that odd flicker in her eyes
and she was gone.

Several days later I had a call from the local police department.
"Mr. Robinson, do you know a Joan————?" he inquired.

"Why do you ask?"

"She took some sleeping pills last night. Someone at her motel
thought she was acting strange and alerted the room clerk who
found her unconscious and called a doctor. This morning she asked
for you and gave me this number to call."

"Officer, I'm afraid the woman is mentally disturbed. There's
nothing I can do to help her. I suggest you get in touch with her
family."

"We'll try to do that, Mr. Robinson." The officer hung up.

I had learned my lesson about fans. But not all letters were from
nuts or proposals of marriage or simpering words of praise for
my performance as Caligula. Some were from people who called
themselves Christians, and some were from Jews. For the most
part they wrote that they sensed a darkness overwhelming my spirit.
One such warning sounded like something my grandmother used
to read out of the Bible.

"Ever since seeing *The Robe* I have been troubled about you.
The hate you showed for Christians in the film must stem from
something that happened to you in real life. In His book God warns
you as follows (Lev. 26:18–20):

> *And if ye will not . . . hearken unto me, then I will punish you seven
> times more for your sins. And I will break the pride of your power;
> and I will make your heaven as iron, and your earth as brass; And
> your strength shall be spent in vain.*"

7

Downhill in a
Gold Cadillac

"JAY ROBINSON WHO made such a hit in 'The Robe' and 'Demetrius and the Gladiators' will play the role of Lord Chadwick with Bette Davis in 'The Virgin Queen'," wrote Louella Parsons in her column.

I felt my waiting was over, but when I got the script, I was very disappointed. It was a standard court villain role. Even so, I had a good rapport with Bette Davis whom I idolized and one afternoon she brought her little daughter, B. D., to my house to see the monkeys. I saved the glass from which Bette Davis drank and her lipstick-stained cigarette ends.

With production completed on *The Virgin Queen* my pleas to Twentieth Century Fox to release me from my contract to work elsewhere were heard. Two years and four months after signing me to play in *The Robe,* my contract was terminated. On August 7, 1955, I received my last paycheck.

My fan mail was still rolling in and there was recognition everywhere I went, but I was typecast as Caligula. The role had taken over the actor. I was like a live butterfly, pinned to a display panel to exhibit its colorful design but unable to move in search of freedom. I began changing agents as often as my shirt.

Finally I was offered a meaty role in a low budget picture, *The Wild Party.* Anthony Quinn was the star and I was to play a junkie named Gage Freeposter. This film, a forerunner to the beatniks and drug culture of the sixties, was so loaded with counter-culture jargon that a printed glossary of terms was handed out at the theatres playing *The Wild Party*. This supposed aid to understanding was a publicity-promotion tool to start people talking about the film.

Gage was a fear-ridden, switchblade-wielding, vicious addict. A real guttersnipe. I poured all the evil I could into the character, completely unaware of how much of the role was seeping into my soul. Anthony Quinn played a former football star, while Kathryn Grant (who later married Bing Crosby) was his girlfriend. At the end of the film, Quinn threw me through a window. My exit line was a craven scream: "I can't stand pain."

Up to this point in my life I had not smoked. The director handed me a carton of cigarettes and said, "Gage is a chain smoker, so you'll have to smoke. Practice with these." I did so and soon found myself craving tobacco.

Then they changed the character, making Gage a nonsmoker. But by now I had acquired the habit and at the end of each scene I would dash off the set for a hurried few puffs. My raveled nerves had found their first crutch.

The Wild Party over, I again began playing musical chairs with agents. There was very little money coming in, but the mounting expenses of my glass mansion continued. Troubles began to pile in on me.

An operation on my mother's lungs revealed a large growth on the chest wall which turned out to be cancer of the lymphatic system. "Terminal," the doctors told me. But a long, lingering illness for mother was followed by frequent surgery and radiation. I kept the truth of her condition from her.

The parties on Stone Canyon continued, but the calibre of my guests dropped as my status dwindled. The top stars stopped coming altogether. There were no interviews now, no personal appearance tours and the phone ceased ringing.

Then came a role in a remake of the Carole Lombard–William Powell comedy, *My Man Godfrey*, this time with June Allyson and David Niven. Henry Koster, director of *The Robe* and *Virgin Queen*, was at the helm. I was offered the part that had made Mischa Auer famous in the earlier version. I was also required to sing, "Lovely-Lovely," a duet with a howling bloodhound. Caligula was now reduced to singing with a dog.

Then came a new blow. My father had gone to his Van Heusen contacts earlier to raise money for my two Broadway productions. All of them had lost on their investments. As a result, my father's influence in the firm began to decline. He was moved to smaller and smaller offices until finally he was forced to resign. He took an executive job in another firm at one-half his previous salary.

With my father's economic losses, he could only look after his second family and had nothing to spare for my mother. Now drained by her medical bills, and with virtually no income of my own, I was overwhelmed with money problems. My bank account was a pitiful remnant of my former wealth.

Friends who had eagerly attended my parties didn't answer my phone calls or seemed vague and distant when we met. In fear and despair, I had no one to turn to and sank deeper into loneliness.

I had a gardener who came weekly to keep the grounds in order. One day, desperate for company of any kind, I heard him clipping a hedge outside a window and stepped out the door to talk to him.

We discussed the weather and other inconsequentials. Then, glancing at me perceptively, he pulled a short, thin cigarette from his pocket and offered it. "Ever try one of these?" he asked. It was the first time I had seen marijuana since that night in the Havana bordello in 1953.

I was curious. After a few puffs, the specter of failure that had been haunting my every waking minute lifted. Plants looked greener, the sky above me melted into a delightful blue. I went inside for a dish of ice cream and it was a feast of cool sweetness. I turned on the hi-fi, and suddenly I was able to enjoy music again, instead of hearing only the frantic beat of my own despair.

The effects of my first marijuana cigarette soon wore off, leaving me in a now-familiar depressed state of mind and craving the fleeting peace I had just enjoyed. I could hardly wait until the gardener returned.

"How did you like it?" he asked when I saw him again.

"Wonderful," I replied. "Where can I get some more?"

He gave me the three joints he had with him but charged me nothing.

At first I did not have to smoke a whole joint to soar high above the trees. A couple of drags would do it. With no work to occupy my time and energy, I was soon living from one joint to the next.

Back in 1957, it was a serious felony to have marijuana in your possession. Not wanting to be caught, every drive in my car to pick up a supply became a nightmare; every policeman posed a threat.

Thanksgiving, Christmas and New Year's passed in a haze. The edges of everything were blurred, indistinct, and I no longer had to think of all the unpleasant things happening to me. I lost interest in the house and neglected it badly. I dropped contact with my agent and stopped looking for roles.

By now I was buying marijuana by the "lid," about one ounce, enough for about fifty joints. I was practically chain smoking the stuff. My Bel Air house became the scene of pot parties and in turn I was invited to others. We would all sit on the floor and exchange meaningful looks at each other. At the time it seemed to have a whole world of significance. At beach parties I would lie in a warm, comfortable sun that caressed my skin, on sand that seemed as soft as silk.

I became the court jester of our crowd. Turned on, I would get up and perform in drug-induced hilarity, and soon everyone was laughing and enjoying the impromptu acts. Even while stoned, the actor in me would emerge and the performance begin.

But eventually the marijuana high did not suffice. Needing something with a bigger kick, I went on to pills, both stimulants and depressants. Soon I was going from Dexedrine uppers to Nembutal downers in various combinations, becoming frequently disoriented in the process.

Then came an offer to do a play in San Francisco at a small theatre on Geary Street called the Encore with a seating capacity of four hundred. The salary—$500 a week. The play was my own story, *Buy Me Blue Ribbons*. The theatre owner flattered me with descriptions of my legions of fans in San Francisco. Eager to get away from Hollywood, I accepted.

My previous visits to San Francisco had been at the expense of Twentieth Century Fox and were orchestrated by professional publicists. I had been ensconced in a lavish suite at the Mark Hopkins, high on Nob Hill, with a panoramic view of beautiful San Francisco Bay. My slightest wish had been instantly gratified. This time I moved into a small commercial hotel that was much less glamorous. On previous visits I had been under my own control; now I was constantly under the influence of pot and pills.

When I threw my back out during rehearsals, I looked around for something to ease the pain. A stagehand named Al offered help. He had just happened to mention that he was the source of drugs for comedian Lenny Bruce who was appearing at a nearby night club.

Al returned with a folded paper containing some white powder. I had asked for codeine tablets but he said this was "something better."

I looked at the powder. There was not much of it and I didn't know how to use it.

"Do I swallow it?" I asked him.

"No," he replied, "sniff it up your nostrils."

I had been introduced to heroin.

Later Al took me to Lenny Bruce's hotel room after the show. By then Lenny was already an addict whose conversation was riddled with obscenities.

I was sniffing the white powder when Lenny, already under the influence of heroin, peered at me through half-closed lids. "That's no way to get high," he said through his stupor. He took the powder, placed it in a spoon with water and a small piece of cotton, heated it with a match and drew it up into a small syringe. Tying a tourniquet around my arm, he had me open and close my fist until the veins on my arm were distended. Then: "I'm gonna put this in your vein where it belongs."

Lenny inserted the needle but couldn't find the vein. He kept pushing the needle around trying to find it, taking it out and starting all over again, until my arm was black and blue with bruises. With a curse he finally gave up in disgust. Years later Lenny died from an overdose of drugs and became a cult figure.

Our play received excellent reviews from the San Francisco critics, but my "legions of San Francisco fans" did not appear. The show closed a big loser at the end of the run. I returned to Los Angeles unaware that I was in bondage now to a daily packet of powder.

When I became violently sick I realized that I must be going through withdrawal. Alarmed, I decided to give up heroin. But I did not give up my drug-centered friends.

One night a friend brought in a car-trunk full of peyote buttons from Texas. This is what some Indians use for hallucinating during religious ceremonies. So we staged a big peyote party. Some fifty of the large, round, flattish-green pods were cut up and boiled down. The process was repeated several times, with the fluid being strained between each boiling, until we were left with a soft block of asphalt-like goo.

All twenty of us lined up and took a spoonful each. Some took two spoons. Not feeling anything after twenty minutes, I swallowed my third spoonful, the others looking on in horror.

The walls began closing in. A friend across the room suddenly took on the appearance of a fearful monster. Fangs grew from his snarling lips and hair began to sprout all over his face. He developed evil, pink, pig-like eyes. I cringed in terror.

The house cat now looked like a tiger, predatory and deadly. Colors leaped at me from the furniture. Menacing faces glared at me from all directions. In a panic I ran out into the safety of the garden, but everything soon became even worse.

Trees reached out at me with hideously gnarled fingers and the moon came plummeting down on me. I hurried back into the house terrified and babbling like a lunatic.

At this stage I didn't know who I was and in blind anxiety found myself lying huddled up in the corner like a fetus, retreating into an imaginary womb for safety.

I exerted all my willpower to tell myself—"You are J-A-Y R-O-B-I-N-S-O-N," spelling the letters carefully for emphasis. Through sheer will power I was coming out of it, but each time I relaxed, the hallucinations flooded back worse than ever.

"Give me something," I pleaded. "Give me something to stop this." No one could or would help me and I had to hold on and wait it out. I didn't remember going home and suffered the terrible effects for a week. Everything frightened me.

I went back to pills to dull my senses. Marijuana was definitely not strong enough for me now. I had left it far behind.

As the months passed, I fell in with a harder crowd, and before I knew what was happening, found myself back on heroin again.

Then one night at a party I saw a striking young blonde woman who looked like someone I knew. But who? I reviewed the actresses whom I had met. No—none of those.

I moved to a corner of the noisy, smoke-filled room and stared. I still couldn't place her. Then she saw me.

"Jay!" she exclaimed. With eyes shining she rushed up to me and threw her arms around my neck. "I've been hoping to find you for months now."

Then I remembered. Pat! The dancer I had swooned over at age 14 in Miami Beach. "You've changed your hair," I stammered.

She laughed. "I've been a blonde for years, Jay. And you became a movie star."

As I looked more closely at Pat, I realized that the past fourteen years had changed her appearance in other ways. There were hard lines around her eyes and mouth. Her skin was sallow.

Still I was attracted to her—almost as strongly as before. I learned she was unmarried, still dancing for a living in a studio and obviously a part of the drug culture. We went home together that night to my Bel Air mansion. The four years difference in our ages didn't matter now.

Weeks later (or was it months?) I was moving languidly about my home one morning, straightening up things after a pot party. Pat was in the living room watching television. The phone rang. It was one of our crowd, a young actor who said he needed a fix. Could I help him? I told him to come on over.

A knock came at the door. It was the young man who had called me.

Taking him into the bathroom, I opened a packet of powder and fixed us both a shot. He then went to the front door and stepped outside for a moment. "What a beautiful day!" he cried as he returned, leaving the door ajar.

The three of us were sitting in the living room when we heard the sound of feet pounding on the driveway and up the steps of redwood rounds. The door was slammed back with a thunderous crash as a horde of men with guns drawn poured into the room.

I found myself staring into the muzzle of one of them. A voice barked at me. "Don't move. You're under arrest. Los Angeles Police Department. Narcotics squad."

I opened my mouth, but nothing would come out. I was numb with shock.

The police searched me and handcuffed my hands behind me. They did the same to Pat. The young man, however, was not hand-cuffed. That puzzled me.

When the police searched the house for evidence, they found the drugs in the bathroom where I had left them. I denied they were mine, said they had been planted there.

Two policemen took me into the bedroom and offered me a deal. No publicity and probably probation, they said, if I would lead them to my dealer. My pride and a false code of honor kept me silent.

The two played a game with me. They used no violence, but one played tough and threatened me with terrible results if I did not lead them to the dealer. The other acted the nice guy and encouraged me to help the police, saying he would help me in return. I continued to deny knowing anything about the drugs they found.

"All right, Mr. Movie Star," growled the heavy, "we're gonna throw the book at you. We're taking you down to the West Holly-wood police station."

Terrified, all I could think to say was, "You'll ruin my career. My mother is dying."

The police led me out of the house, handcuffed and dazed. As I left, one of the officers was studying the press stories in my scrap-book. He turned to me as I passed, hand pointing to the most recent page of clippings. "That's the last page you'll need for this book," he said.

Mutely, I just nodded my head.

A line of unmarked police cars stood along the street outside my house. The neighbors were all out on their lawns gawking as one of the more famous residents was led out of his house in hand-cuffs, face crimson with embarrassment. Pat and the young actor were taken off in a separate police car.

At the West Hollywood station I was booked, fingerprinted, and mug shots were taken of me. My belt and shoe laces were removed and I was led to my cell, holding up my pants with one hand.

A solid steel door slammed shut behind me with terrible finality.

Caligula was behind bars.

8

Reunion

MY FIRST NIGHT in a jail cell was spent in fear and sleeplessness. Shortly before dawn I called out for the jailer. No answer. Then I took off a shoe and banged loudly on the door until the clanging filled the corridor outside.

Still no one came, so I redoubled my efforts. Around me vague cries of protest, as if from disembodied voices, arose from prisoners in other cells.

An eye suddenly appeared, framed by the peep hole in my door. It regarded me with a baleful, deliberate stare. Feeling like some specimen on a microscope slide, I stopped banging and stood hesitantly facing the door, shoe still clasped in my hand.

A voice thrust itself upon me roughly. "What's all the uproar?"

"Please help me," I said. "This is my first offense and I was framed."

"They all say that! If you didn't do anything, why are you in here?"

"I don't know. Can I make a phone call?"

The guard opened the door. "Who do you want to call?"

I thought of my mother, or the nurse looking after her. But how could either one help? "Who can I call?" I asked desperately.

"A lawyer or a bail bondsman," was the reply.

I didn't know either, so I looked up a bail bondsman who had a 24-hour number.

A sleepy male voice asked a few questions, not caring if I was innocent or guilty, just what kind of collateral I had. When he heard I owned a Bel Air house, the barricades fell like magic. "We'll have you out by tomorrow morning," was the last thing I heard.

A lawyer sent by the bail bondsman came to see me and, as promised, I tottered out of the police station into the glare of the California sun later the same day. The lawyer took me to a hamburger joint on the Sunset Strip. Afterwards, as I stepped out onto Sunset Boulevard, a line of coin-in-the-slot newspaper dispensers revealed screaming banner headlines:

"BEL AIR MANSION RAIDED"
"MAD EMPEROR ARRESTED ON NARCOTICS CHARGES"
"STAR OF RELIGIOUS FILM ARRESTED ON DRUG CHARGE"

My world crumbled anew. Dashing round the corner I threw up in the weeds, leaning against a wooden fence, pale, weak and shaking. Then the lawyer drove me to Bel Air and back to the sanctuary of my own home.

Later that afternoon he came by to get more details. But I still lived in a fantasy world. I didn't really know this man. Why should I open up to him? Why should I tell him intimate, embarrassing facts about myself? And so I lied.

I pretended I never took drugs. Someone planted them in my house, I declared angrily. In fact, I was almost beginning to believe it myself, so deep was my self-delusion.

I learned later that Pat and the young actor had not been booked and were released soon after being taken into custody. Nor did their names appear in any press stories. It was all "Mad Emperor" coverage. I was the lone heavy!

Reluctant to appear anywhere in public, I stayed indoors in a daze. The ruins of my life hung about me like the tattered clothing of a derelict. What would the newspaper stories do to my mother and father?

The next day I had mercifully disappeared from the headlines. Tyrone Power had died in Spain from a heart attack. It was a respite from publicity for me, as Power's death was a big loss to the film capital. Mother, I found, hadn't learned about my arrest; her nurse had kept the news from her.

Deeply shaken by the experience, I craved drugs even more. When I phoned my dealer, he greeted me warmly having heard somehow that I had not cooperated with the police. "You're a stand-up guy," he enthused. Later I wondered what exactly I had stood up for.

My appearance in Beverly Hills Municipal Court was uneventful. I was arraigned under Section 11500 of the California Penal Code on several counts of possession of narcotics—a felony. If convicted, I could get a sentence of one to ten years in state prison. Even during my court appearance I was propped up by the needle.

Legal maneuvering by my lawyer delayed my next appearance, for a preliminary hearing, until January 1959. Just before Christmas I phoned Dad in New York. "I need you now more that I ever did before in my life. Can I come and spend Christmas with you?" I pleaded.

As always Dad was quick to help. I went out to the airport and caught the first available flight. When Dad met me at the airport, I reeled under the impact of the changes in him. All my life I had looked up to this handsome, assured executive who had been so esteemed by his contemporaries. Now he was stripped of his status. I really saw him for the first time—a graying man near 60, deep lines in his angular face from the pummeling of life, the confident light gone from his brown eyes.

When he first saw me at the airport, I could tell by his expression that Dad was even more appalled at the changes in my appearance.

We spent Christmas together in a small suite he had rented in a New York apartment hotel; he knew I would find it awkward staying with his second family on Long Island. During these few days together we became closer than ever before. I wished that I had known him better through the years now gone. We needed each other, both having suffered loss of pride and material success and personal esteem.

Christmas day we spent together in his plain hotel suite: a small living room with two worn brown chairs, a sofa with a green-striped slipcover, and a tiny kitchenette in one corner. The bedroom was small with twin beds, one chest of drawers, a table and two straight chairs. I wondered if he borrowed money to pay for it.

Holding to his Jewish faith, Dad didn't celebrate the birth of Jesus; since I had no faith at all this was fine with me. As we talked and Dad smoked one cigar after another, I suddenly realized that he had a dependency too. His cigars seemed to keep his emotions under control.

When I described Mother's deterioration, I saw a tear slowly trickle down his cheek. Suddenly I realized he still loved her.

By the second day my craving for drugs was too much for me. "Dad, there's something I need to tell you," I said slowly. "I'm really hooked on drugs."

I watched the color slowly drain from his face and felt a shaft of remorse that I was now responsible for one more deep hurt in his life. He didn't say anything for a long moment. "How bad is it?" he asked.

"Bad enough that I need something right away," I said desperately, my face drawn, mouth tight, hands clasping and unclasping. Sweat was starting to form across my eyebrows and upper lip.

"What can I do?" he asked helplessly.

"Get me to a doctor who can write a prescription for me."

He shook his head. "There's got to be a better way."

My hands were beginning to sweat now. "If you don't do something, I'll have to fly back to California for my supply."

With great heaviness, he went to the telephone and called his personal doctor. An awkward conversation followed, then an appointment was made for the following morning. I didn't see how I could get through the night, but somehow I did. My father didn't sleep much either, getting up to put an extra blanket on me when he saw me shivering. Near dawn, when I was shaking so hard the bed trembled, he came over and held my hand.

Dad's doctor looked me over carefully the next morning, asked some questions, then gave me a prescription which kept me going through the holidays.

We spent New Year's Eve in the hotel room, watching television. At midnight Guy Lombardo welcomed 1959 with *Auld Lang Syne* and we could hear the sounds of cheering multitudes from nearby Times Square filtering through our windows. We had nothing to celebrate. Our good days, such as they were, seemed far behind.

I got up to turn the television off but stood there in front of it, not wanting to face the silent drabness of the room. My father arose from his chair, laid his cigar down and came over beside me. Hesitantly, he reached over and patted my shoulder.

Something broke inside me. I began to sob. His arm reached around my shoulders and I clung to him. As the country celebrated the new year, the two of us stood there, arms wrapped around each other, patting each other awkwardly yet tenderly. It was the first real communication we had ever experienced; just two desolate men without pretensions who loved each other.

My father began to cry, rivers of tears running down his gaunt cheeks, the drops spattering over his nose and down his chin. My heart wrenched and I too began to cry. Dad rocked me in his arms, sobbing for his son for whom he had hoped so much.

Consumed by sorrow, guilt and grief over so many hurts, a love came swelling out of our hearts like the strains of some magnificent old pipe organ. It was to be our closest moment.

The next morning Dad took me to the airport. He insisted on carrying my suitcase and my heart bled as I watched this formerly vigorous man struggle with one small piece of luggage. But I would not injure the little pride he had left by taking it from him. So each in his own way plodded through the airport.

When we said good-by Dad looked white, haggard and very old. Aboard the plane, I took a seat so that I could look out the window and see my father. He was standing at the ramp looking so fragile that my heart sank.

As the plane edged away from its dock and turned toward the runway, I saw him waving.

I never saw my father again.

9

Descent into Hell

MY PRELIMINARY HEARING in the Santa Monica Superior Court
took place soon after my return from New York. The proceedings
moved slowly, voices were low pitched, the words keyed even lower.
Everyone seemed bored but me, for every word spoken had bearing
on whether I would be able to resume life as a free man or find
myself caged as a felon.

When the narcotics officers testified, I learned my telephone had
been bugged. The surprise witness for the prosecution was called—
the young actor who had been there with Pat and me at the time
of our arrest. I thought he was my friend. He never once looked
at me as he testified how it had been prearranged for him to call
out "What a beautiful day!" to the police and then leave the door
open. He told of the telephone conversation in which I had said
there were drugs in the house, how he had directed the police to
the drugs in the bathroom. Each new piece of evidence sounded
like a nail being pounded into my cell door.

My lawyer had been confident of our victory and I, absorbing
it from him, felt I had a very good chance. But I had lied to him
and the unfolding evidence took him by surprise.

The syringe had been found; analysis showed it contained a residue
of methadone. A spoon also revealed traces of drugs.

For two weeks I had been paying a large price for what I had
been told was heroin. To my surprise the lab technicians pronounced

75

the contents of the packet in my bathroom to be methadone, a "safe" drug now given legally to addicts in some government-sponsored drug programs. The judge pronounced the evidence sufficient for trial and after legal maneuvering on my lawyer's part, the date of the trial was set.

I staggered from the court like a drunken man. One of my first acts was to call my father in New York at his new place of business to tell him the result of the hearing.

The operator said, "One moment, please." There was a lengthy pause and then a voice came on the line. "I'm sorry. Mr. Robinson died of a heart attack just a few minutes ago."

Numbed, I hung up the phone. It couldn't be! Not after we had discovered how much we loved and needed each other. The warmth that had come into my heart during the New York visit ebbed away. The flicker of light that had entered my soul was extinguished. My dad was gone. It wasn't fair. Once again someone I really cared about had been snatched from me. Self-pity flooded me. I couldn't even cry.

My father's second wife invited me to the funeral, but I had retreated into a mental withdrawal that closed all doors to the outside world. For five months I swam in a sea of dope. Wary of me because of my arrest, dealers made it increasingly hard to obtain drugs, until finally I was forced to go out on the street for pickups. This was a new nether world of crime in which I was naive, totally unsuited to having to fend for myself. The people I was mixing with now would do anything for a fix, including armed robbery or even murder. Nobody trusted anyone else and I walked a tightrope across a yawning canyon of suspicion.

An addict tries to leave a small fix for a wake-up shot the next day. Each morning I would wake up sick, gasping, reaching for that shot to cure my misery. I was filled with only one desire—to plunge the needle deep into my arm and get relief.

During this period I was totally wiped out, like a classroom blackboard from which all chalk impressions had been erased. There was nothing for me but blackness. The only thing I looked forward to in life was the next fix.

Pat reappeared full of compassion and sympathy. The police, she said, were probably watching my every move. If I had any money in the bank I should withdraw it at once. In view of my impending trial, I should beware of possible creditors attaching my account. At her suggestion, I withdrew my remaining savings of $3,400 and Pat and I took off for a nearby resort motel. The next morning I groggily heard Pat say that she was going out for breakfast. Dazedly I turned over to resume sleep.

A knock came at the door. I ignored it. The knocking continued. "Is that you, Pat?" I called out. Louder knocking was the only answer.

I got up and opened the door. A large, hulking man stood there, a stocking pulled down over his face, flattening his nose and distorting his features. With a violent shove, he pushed me inside and onto the floor. The door was kicked shut behind him.

"Where's the money?"

My blood chilled. What was happening to me now?

We fought all over the room. I struggled desperately but was no match for his strength. As we wrestled I managed to pull off his stocking mask and recognized the man as a friend of Pat's whom I had seen at Bel Air pot parties.

He found all the money, pocketed the bills and growled from the doorway: "Tell the police and I'll kill you!"

I sat there for awhile not knowing what to do. Once again I had been betrayed by someone I cared about. To Pat I was nothing but an easy set-up. Pat and her friend had probably figured that with my trial coming up, I would keep my mouth shut. Bitterness flooded me. I didn't care anymore. Was there anyone left who would not betray me? I called the police and reported the robbery.

In the morning the headlines shouted:

"ACTOR BEATEN AND ROBBED BY MASKED BANDIT."

I was in the news again and once more the details of my drug arrest were rehashed as part of the story. Later Pat and her friend were picked up together in Florida and held there in jail, then released later when I did not press charges. I was too immersed in my own difficulties at the time. Anyway, the $3,400 probably long since had been spent.

The film colony now treated me like a pariah. Just as the Roman emperor had gone mad nineteen hundred years before, the movie people figured that now the twentieth century Caligula had lost his mind. At the age of 28 I was written off as hopeless.

All through the early gray months of 1959 I trod the slum streets of Los Angeles desperately searching for drugs. And not a week passed in which I was not ripped off in countless ways by the scum of the earth.

A month before the trial my lawyer took a look at the wreckage and told me incredulously, "You can't go to court looking like this."

He sent me to a private sanitarium in Long Beach to recuperate. Then he hired a hefty male nurse as a guard so I couldn't sneak out and damage myself all over again. Doctors put me on a program of withdrawal through tranquilizers to offset the terrible pains and sickness that followed. I slept the days away as my body threw off the residue of the drugs. Massive doses of vitamins were given to build me up.

When it was time to return to Santa Monica for the jury trial, my body was restored somewhat and I was wearing a new suit. But I still took sleeping pills at night and stimulants and tranquilizers during the day to get through the ordeal. The male nurse stayed at my side throughout the trial.

My lawyer did his best, but he was not a criminal lawyer. The case against me unfolded grimly and methodically. My betrayer reappeared and told his story, adding his weight to the relentless thrusts of the prosecutor.

My plea had been not guilty, though there was certainly enough evidence to convict me. When I took the stand in my own defense, I again repeated the lies which I had consistently told since the narcotics officers first broke into my house.

In his summation the prosecutor placed great emphasis on my

roles in both *The Robe* and *Demetrius and the Gladiators.* "This man was a star in religious pictures who was looked up to by millions. He has betrayed that position," he snapped. "The films brought inspiration to millions, but he's brought dishonor and shame to his profession." I felt pierced by the contemptuous looks all around me.

The jury retired and deliberated interminably. For two and a half days we waited for the verdict. "The longer they take deliberating, the better it is for you," my lawyer confided. "I think they'll find you not guilty."

A call rang out. "The jury is coming back." There was a scamper of feet as everyone resumed their places.

"Have you reached a verdict?" the judge inquired.

"We have, Your Honor," said the foreman of the jury.

"How do you find?"

"Guilty."

The jury of eleven women and one man had turned thumbs down on Caligula.

Before I could even react, the judge immediately intoned, "Remanded to county jail until sentence is passed."

I was taken out the back door and down into the bowels of the courthouse. Handcuffs were snapped on my wrists. Through a large metal eye on the handcuffs ran a chain connecting me to the other prisoners. I was now tied to a group of rapists, murderers and robbers. Having entered the underworld in my search for dope, I was now bound physically to its dregs. My crime—the damage I had done to myself.

Our shambling group was taken to the old county jail which looked and smelled like the dungeon of some medieval fortress, an amalgam of grime-encrusted stone, crumbling brickwork, steel cages badly in need of paint, and, over all, an odious aroma of disinfectant, perspiration and human wastes.

Once inside, we were herded into what is called the holding pen where we joined a multitude of other prisoners. This particular section of the jail was built for far smaller groups than our closely packed mass of stinking humanity. We were huddled together with scarcely room to breathe. Addicts and drunks vomited over themselves; some urinated where they stood. The stench was sickening. By this time the effects of the drugs I had taken earlier in the day had begun to wear off.

A sudden series of electric-like shocks jangled my nerves and sensations crawled over my skin as if insects were scurrying across my body. I was twitching, squirming while a tic beat convulsively in my cheek. Perspiration soaked my clothing as I was gripped by chills and sniffles. I was beginning to withdraw cold turkey.

The experience was literally hell on earth, a scene from the *Lower Depths*. Crowded in among the rapists, addicts and murderers were lost and bewildered young kids. Some were hardly more than teen-agers, staring around them in wide-eyed horror at scenes they could scarcely comprehend.

We were moved to another tank where all our clothes were taken away. Then we were thrust under a shower that deloused as it cleaned. The chemicals smelled like cattle or sheep dip. Meanwhile I was getting sicker and sicker.

In another tank I was searched for concealed objects or drugs. Probes were inserted into every opening on my body until I felt like an animal.

It took twenty-four hours to complete the booking process before I was taken to the tank up on the thirteenth floor. Into cells which had been built for forty-five inmates, a hundred or more of us were crowded. Each cell had double-tiered steel bunks against the wall. Additional prisoners slept on the floor on mattresses. The corridor floor outside the cells, called "the freeway," was also jammed with prisoners sleeping on mattresses. This is where I was assigned.

Could all this really be happening in the beautiful "City of Angels?" Did this horror really exist within a few miles of my luxurious home in Bel Air?

Sleeping was impossible and I lay upon a foul-smelling, lice-infested mattress staring at the ceiling and listening to the barnyard chorus of snorts, grunts and groans from the sleeping prisoners around me. Meanwhile, my withdrawal was getting worse and I was beginning to hallucinate. People's faces were distorted. It was like looking into wavy mirrors in the old-fashioned carnival arcades.

An old man next to me had been crying and twitching badly. I shouted for a guard, but no one came. Finally he just laid there, very still.

The next morning the guards ordered us to stand up. The old man didn't move. He had died in the night. The guards dragged the body away on his mattress, down the corridor, his heels bumping along over the floor.

Nights continued to be filled with the writhing and screaming of tortured souls. After eight days I still had not been able to sleep. On the ninth night, I picked out the biggest man I could find and asked him to punch me out. He refused at first, but I pleaded. Finally, he drew back a huge fist and lights exploded in my head.

I remembered nothing more until I awoke the next morning with a very sore jaw. But the withdrawal agony was broken. From then on I slept at night like the other prisoners, mercifully unaware of their noises.

I slept on that mattress in the corridor for twenty-five days until I was moved into a cell. But my mattress stayed on the cell floor as the bunk beds were occupied. By now I had started to eat normally; after so long without real nourishment, I found myself ravenous for the jail food, poor as it was.

When the probation officer came to see me to make out his report, I told him my mother was dying, my father had just died, and I was a film star who had done nothing to hurt anybody. Since this was my first offense, he decided to recommend straight probation.

After thirty-eight days in the county jail, I was taken back to court for sentencing. My suit, shirt and other garments were returned to me so that I could make a presentable appearance. But I had lost so much weight in jail that my clothes hung loosely.

My lawyer stated that since this was my first offense, he hoped that the judge would want to follow the recommendation of the probation officer.

However, as I stood before the judge, I was shocked to hear him sentence me to one year in the county jail. Stupefied, I was led back to the house of horror in which I had already been suffering for more than a month.

Defeated and hopeless, I lost all sense of time as the days passed.

Then one morning I heard a guard calling out my name. Shuffling after him into the office I was curtly informed that I was to be freed on $2,500 bond pending appeal. My lawyer had gone to another court to plead my case and a different judge had decided to set me free.

A few hours later I was released on a street in downtown Los Angeles not six blocks from where Leo Riley and I had first stepped off the San Diego bus six years before. The wheel had turned full circle.

Top left: Barbara Breslaw Robinson, Jay's mother, shown here dressed for a role on Broadway about 1925. She danced in musical comedies in the 1920s as Bobbie Breslaw. *Top right:* Stanley Robinson, Jay's father, at age 21. *Bottom left:* Jay, age 2, with his maternal grandmother, Etta MacDonald Breslaw. She was a loving woman who tried to interest the child in God, but her death served only to alienate the future Caligula from a loving Father. *Bottom right:* Jay at age 11 with his mother. The picture was taken in 1941 in Miami Beach.

Above: Stanley Robinson, Jay's father, in his office at Van Heusen, about 1948. *Below:* Jay in the title role in *Gayden* with Fay Bainter, 1949. This was one of the early roles that helped establish him as a Broadway star. He was 19 at the time.

Top left: Boris Karloff, left, prepares to "throttle" a believably frightened Jay Robinson in *The Shop at Sly Corner,* 1949. It was Jay's Broadway debut and although the play was panned by critics, Robinson was singled out time and again for praise. *Top right:* Jay Robinson, age 19, and already a star on Broadway. *Center:* Now 21, Jay is shown in *Buy Me Blue Ribbons,* a New York play he also produced with money given him by his father. Financing the production helped ruin his father and the play was mercilessly criticized in the newspapers. *Bottom:* Jay with Katharine Hepburn, left, and Cloris Leachman, costumed for the Theatre Guild's revival of Shakespeare's *As You Like It* in January 1950.

Above: A famous scene from *The Robe*—Richard Burton as Marcellus and Jean Simmons as Diana stand before their emperor, Caligula (Jay Robinson), to be sentenced for crimes of conspiracy and sedition in connection with their Christian faith. *Left:* Jay as Caligula and Susan Hayward as Messalina in *Demetrius and the Gladiators,* 1954. *Right:* Victor Mature as Demetrius hands the robe of Jesus of Nazareth to a frightened Caligula in *Demetrius and the Gladiators.* (Photos courtesy of Twentieth Century-Fox.)

Left: Jay, with pet gibbon ape, in front of his BelAir mansion during the height of his Caligula fame—1954. Monkeys and apes were kept as pets in cages located behind the mansion. *Right:* Jay as Lord Chadwick with Bette Davis, during filming of *The Virgin Queen* in 1955.

Jay Robinson, once hailed as a Hollywood "genius," sits in empty BelAir mansion surrounded by posters and scrapbooks. At left is portrait of him in *The Robe*. The other at the right was painted by Katharine Hepburn. (Los Angeles *Times* photo, 11/27/59.)

Jay Robinson sits dejected and alone in a Santa Monica courtroom, awaiting the jury's verdict in his trial on narcotic charges. (Los Angeles *Times* Photo 5/13/59.)

10

Enter Pauline

ON JUNE 23, 1959, I stood on a busy street corner in downtown Los Angeles. It was evening and I felt strange amid the flashing neon signs. For the time being I was free. My general health was better because I had been off drugs for six weeks. But where to go? I had no family or friends except a dying mother. Rather than go to her now, I decided to get myself in better shape first.

My Bel Air home was empty, desolate and full of bad memories, but it was all I had. A cab dropped me off in front. The sight of it made me sick. I am a lover of plants and shrubs, of animals and anything alive; my garden had once been a jungle of lush tropical growth, green and beautiful. Now the verdant greenery was brown and dried up from lack of water and care. My jungle was dead; it was symbolic of my life.

When I moved back into the house, everything inside it was dead as well. No one came near me, the telephone did not ring and the only sign of life was the mailbox. It was stuffed with overdue bills and circulars.

I discovered that my mother was now in Burlingame, California, staying with an old friend. She was literally being burned alive with massive doses of radiation and injections of nitrogen mustard. My once beautiful mother who loved life so much was reduced to a living death.

I felt my own mortality threatened. With nothing to do or look forward to doing, it was inevitable that once more I reach for something to blot out my emotional and spiritual pain. And then perhaps the most bizzare episode of this whole period of my life occurred.

My lawyer called with a suggestion. "I've heard about a new program to help addicts and alcoholics," he said. "And it's free."

I was intrigued. "What's it all about?"

"It's a psychological program to short-circuit lengthy analysis and provide fast answers for the causes of addiction."

"How does it work?"

"They give you some pills which allow the doctor to go deep into the subconscious and get rid of your craving for drugs."

"What pills?"

"Lysergic acid," was the reply. I had never heard of it. This was years before LSD became a household catch phrase.

I was taken to a psychiatrist's office in West Los Angeles. I have no memory of his name or address. Before the treatments began, I had to sign a release freeing the doctor of responsibility if anything went wrong. Then I was given four little blue pills and tightly strapped down onto an examining table.

Music began to play and I recognized it with horror. It was a death march. The great lone bass drum beat at the end of each passage knocked upon the gates of my psyche as though the devil with a sharp-pronged pitchfork was trying to gain admission to my soul. The doctor began questioning me just as the hallucinations started.

I writhed against restraining straps while demons and goblins chased me all over the globe. I had five lengthy sessions like this. At the end of each one a handful of tranquillizers were given me to bring me down from my terror. Nothing positive came out of these frightening trips and after the fifth session I refused to go back.

Who paid for these experiments? Were they officially sanctioned? If so, by whom? Surely no doctor would do this on his own, for where was the profit that would offset such tremendous risks?

Were these experiments part of a university-conducted series of such tests? Or were they part of an attempt at mind control?

I have no answers; and the questions only raise more questions.

As a befuddled addict, I had been recruited to be a guinea pig and deliberately led down a terrible path into the gaping mouth of hell.

The months passed in a daze and I returned to my old sources for drugs. In July I took a second trust deed on the house since the balance in my bank account had disappeared. It all went down the needle of a syringe. The habit now was stronger than ever and the mortgage money was spent quickly. I sold my car, and when that money had been spent, my mother's car as well.

My $300 custom-made suits disappeared into a downtown pawn shop where they fetched me $10 each. My shoes, the hi-fi set and an extensive record collection followed rapidly.

One day while I was home, knocked out on drugs, somebody entered the house and ransacked it. Several days later I saw an advertisement in the paper for a company that purchased used furniture. I made a call. A man soon came to the house to evaluate what was left of the beautiful collection of furnishings that had cost me more than $30,000.

"How much cash will you give me for the lot?" I asked.

"A thousand dollars," he replied.

I agreed, on the condition that he'd leave me one mattress so I would have something to sleep on, and one lamp so I could see at night. Its shade became a dirty towel.

Thanksgiving Day of 1959 arrived. What was there to give thanks for? The house was stripped; the utilities had all been cut off; for water I had filled the bathtub and this supply was diminishing fast. The taxes on the house had not been paid. Only the telephone was left as a link with the outside world, but it too would be cut off soon. Late one afternoon while talking to the telephone operator I passed out. She notified the police.

The sound of pounding at the front door roused me from my stupor and staggering to my feet I opened the door. It was a patrolman together with a writer-photographer team from the *Los Angeles Times*. Someone had tipped off the *Times* that I was a good human interest story.

I was a wreck. My hair was uncut and tousled, my face stubbled with beard. A dirty shirt hung on my shoulders and the house was empty and dark without electricity.

My soul and spirit were dead, but not my ego. Caligula had retained his scrapbook when all else was gone. The reporters spread the pages of clippings around me on the floor of the great empty living room. Behind me they placed one of my few remaining possessions—an oil painting of me as Caligula with the two little horns protruding from my head in satanic fashion.

The next day an eight-column banner picture dominated the front page. Headlines again screamed frantic words back at me: "HOLLY-WOOD'S FORGOTTEN GENIUS FOUND DESTITUTE IN BEL AIR MANSION." At the time I had just $13.69 left in the world.

Paul Coates had a hard-hitting news and human interest show on a local TV channel. He invited me to appear. I told my story and money trickled in from little people all over the city until it amounted to $1,200. I went right out and spent it on drugs.

My memory is hazy as to how I finally lost the house. There still was some equity in it and someone offered me a small sum to sign a paper. I did so in my muddled disorientation. With no income there was no way I could make payments on three mortgages. The vultures had picked the last piece of flesh from the bones of Caligula.

But the closing out of this phase of my life produced a change in me. I was somehow lighter, freer, even though the drug craving remained. Something more than my possessions had been removed.

Somehow it all led me to make a decision. I will never forget the date—January 19, 1960. Until then I had hurt only myself. But I knew that if I was to continue using drugs I would eventually hurt someone else.

Even in my hazy state, I knew I was at a crossroads. It was up to me to decide which way to go.

On that day I entered a small private hospital which provided a withdrawal program. I had known of this place before but never had the will to go there. Strangely, now I did.

I went through withdrawal for a week. It was like lying in the bowels of an inferno. Nothing stayed in my stomach. I lost all control of body functions as little evil things with pitchforks kept prodding and jabbing me. But when I left that hospital, I felt I was free of the addiction. To this day I don't know how the hospital was paid, or even if it was paid.

And then a series of events followed which changed my life.

I got a room at the inexpensive Knickerbocker Hotel. Worried about how I was going to pay my bill there, I went to the Bank of America branch at the corner of Hollywood Boulevard and Cahuenga. I was trying to negotiate a loan when I was suddenly overtaken by wracking chest pains. I was afraid it might be my heart. The loan officer insisted on finding me a doctor. He pulled out a list of bank-approved physicians and made a call. The first doctor could not see me; he took only insurance cases.

The loan officer picked a second number. A nurse answered and said they could take no further patients that day.

"But this man has chest pains and should see a doctor right now!" urged the loan officer.

"Send him over right away then," came the reply.

The loan officer insisted he accompany me. Together we walked east along Hollywood Boulevard to the American Airlines building on the northeast corner of Hollywood and Vine. The numbers chiseled into the stonework over the building were 6253.

An elevator took us up to the eighth floor and on the frosted glass panel of the medical office was stenciled "L. DALE HUFFMAN, M.D."

As we entered a tastefully furnished reception room, I was suddenly faced by a vision of gentleness. She wore a starched white uniform and white nurse's cap. Her long black hair was parted in the middle of her head and severely pulled back over her ears.

There was a moment of what seemed to be recognition between us—as if we already knew each other. I was hardly aware of the loan officer, or of his leaving, and almost forgot the chest pain. She came out from behind the built-in cubicle where her desk was and asked, "Are you in pain now?"

Her eyes were almost moist with concern and she seemed both soft and firm as a rock at the same time.

When I said I felt a little better, she smiled, and suggested that I go into the examination room and lie down. She took my arm. Although she was slight, her hand was firm. I felt safe, protected. Strangely enough the pain left.

Before I lay down on the examining table, she asked me to take off my sweater and shirt. "The doctor wants me to do an EKG," she said.

"What's that?" I asked.

"Oh, it's just a graph reading of your heart rate and its impulses. It doesn't hurt."

Slowly and hesitantly I took off my sweater and then my shirt. Suddenly I was ashamed of my hideously bruised, scarred and scabbed arms. The nurse looked at my arms, and then directly into my eyes. Her big dark eyes were so sad I thought she was going to cry.

"You poor man, what have you done to yourself?" There wasn't judgment or reproach in her voice. I felt that she was deeply hurt by my pain and suffering. This compassionate woman in white truly cared.

For the first time in many years a flicker of softness nudged the hardness of my heart.

11

Monkey off My Back

THE EKG REVEALED a rapid heartbeat and Dr. Huffman sensed that my problems were more emotional than medical. "You're run down. Stay off drugs. Get some exercise. Eat regularly. Build up your body," he advised. "Better come back tomorrow morning. We'll have a report by then on your blood test."

With the examination over, I found myself not wanting to leave Dr. Huffman's office. In here I was safe and secure; outside lurked terrible danger. So I sat quietly in the waiting room. The doctor soon left and the nurse looked at me, her eyes troubled.

"Do you feel well enough to leave?" she asked.

"No, I really don't. Can I sit here for awhile?" I asked pleadingly.

"I guess so," she said.

"Would you tell me your name?"

"It's Pauline—Pauline Flowers."

"I like the name Pauline; it suits you," I said reflectively. "Would you please call me Jay?"

She nodded and turned back to some paperwork on her desk, but I could not take my eyes off her. I had encountered many of Hollywood's most glamorous women, but Pauline had something they all lacked. What was it? Her face had a delicate, piquant quality. Her smile was warm, her mouth gentle. But it was the deep compassion in her large brown eyes that pierced my heart. Or was it an unusual inner beauty I sensed?

As I sat staring at her, she looked up at me several times with a question in her eyes.

"Do you mind if I stay a few more minutes?" I would ask.

It was almost six o'clock when she stood up and came over to me. "I'm sorry, but I really have to close the office now."

"Please sit down here for a few minutes," I said. "I need to talk to someone."

She hesitated a moment, then sat down. "Why don't you want to leave, Jay?"

"I think it's because you're here."

"But I have to go home now. We can't just sit here."

I sighed. "Will you do me a favor?"

"If I can."

"Will you walk to my hotel with me?"

A cloud crossed her face and I hurried on. "I mean, just to the front entrance. It's over on Ivar. It's the Knickerbocker."

She looked at me very directly for a long moment, then nodded. "All right, let's go."

I was surprised at how much strength I suddenly had. It was chilly outside and Pauline had worn a coat. I leaped to help her with it, then opened the door for her. She turned out the lights, slipped on the catch and carefully closed the door to be sure it was locked.

On the way to my hotel I discovered that Pauline knew nothing about me nor had she seen any of my movies. This appealed to me. I was starting out fresh with her.

"You must be a New York actor," she said.

For some reason this also pleased me. "Why do you say that?" I asked.

She thought a moment. "You have more, well, depth than the Hollywood actors who come to our office." In her gentle way she was beginning to restore some of my confidence.

When we arrived at the entrance to my hotel, I didn't want her to leave, so I kept on talking. Seeing that she was ill at ease standing there, I said impulsively, "Will you have dinner with me tonight?"

Once again she searched my eyes thoughtfully. "Tonight will

be difficult for me. I have errands to do, some telephone calls to make . . ."

"We can make it later . . . say eight o'clock."

Another hesitation. "Well, all right."

We met at a Hamburger Hamlet. Afterward, as we walked and talked, she let me hold her hand. I learned she was 27 years old; she had been born in Ada, Oklahoma, the youngest of three children. Her parents were Fletcher and Naomi Flowers. When her parents divorced, Pauline, her sister and mother had moved to California when Pauline was 11. Her father's family belonged to the Holiness Church; her mother was a Baptist. Pauline said she had become a Christian in her teens.

"A Christian?" I laughed. "With a father and mother like that weren't you a Christian from the day you were born?"

Pauline smiled. "I'm sorry. What I mean is I accepted Christ as my personal Savior when I was 14."

I changed the subject. She wore a little pin shaped like a bird and I pointed to it. "Are you a bird lover?"

I discovered she loved all animals—in fact, any creature that was helpless and needy. Pauline's compassionate nature had led her into nursing. I finally took her to her car, a small brown Ford coupe, and watched with deep longing as she drove away.

It was a sleepless night. All my deep needs for someone who could really care for me flooded back. I could hardly wait until morning because I was due back in Dr. Huffman's office at 10 A.M.

When Pauline arrived to open the office at 8:45 the next morning, I was waiting.

"Your appointment is at ten, isn't it?" she asked, perplexed.

"That's right," I said with a grin.

Back came her quick smile. "You'll have to read a magazine or something. There's a woman coming at nine for a physical."

I sat and watched Pauline while she quietly dealt with the imperious socialite who arrived five minutes early, demanding to see the doctor immediately. As a nurse, she was gentle but firm. Every move of her head, every gesture, every word she uttered fascinated me.

Nothing in my blood test changed Dr. Huffman's prescription for me. "You've damaged your body through drugs," he said bluntly. "But the body has marvelous recuperative powers."

Then he dismissed me.

It was only 10:30 A.M. by then. Pauline had been busy with a patient so I sat down and tried to read a magazine. When she came out, she was smiling. "The doctor says you're all right. He prescribes good clean living, regular meals; that sort of thing."

"You can help—by coming to lunch with me."

We made a date for noon and I sat down to wait.

"Jay, you can't just wait here."

"Why not?"

"Dr. Huffman will think it a bit strange." But her eyes were smiling.

"I'll go if you insist, but there's something so peaceful and comforting in this office that I can't bear to leave."

Pauline's eyes softened. Impulsively she reached for my hand. "All right, Jay. But try to read a magazine. When you keep looking at me I get nervous."

During lunch I discovered that she had two boyfriends—one in Arizona and one in Glendale. She was not serious about either one.

That afternoon I went back to the bank. The loan officer was relieved to see that I was all right. When I told him I expected work soon as an actor, he indicated that the loan would go through.

I could hardly wait to tell Pauline. Her eyes lit up when she saw me enter the office. "It's good news," I said. "The loan is going through."

"I'm so glad."

"Will you help me celebrate?"

"How?"

"By going out to dinner with me."

"Oh, Jay. I shouldn't tonight."

"Why not?"

"Well, I . . . okay, but let's make it at eight again."

By now I was completely in love with Pauline. Her sweetness brought me into a new world. Before, all had been blackness; now, with her, life was bright again. That night I kissed her for the first time.

Two nights later we were sitting in the front seat of her small coupe, talking about my plans to go back to the Broadway stage. Suddenly I knew I just could not go on living without her.

"Pauline, will you marry me?"

She looked at me like a startled doe. "But Jay, that's crazy," she protested. "We don't really know each other. And your life is so mixed up."

"All I know is that I don't want to go on living without you," I replied doggedly. "I've never proposed to anyone before, but I'm convinced that you're the one for me, Pauline. And I intend to fight for you. Anything worthwhile is worth fighting for."

Pauline's wide, warm brown eyes studied me thoughtfully. "I do care for you, Jay. But I have to be sure. First, I want to talk to Dr. Huffman. He's been like a father to me."

My heart sank at the bit of news. I could hardly expect a recommendation from this worldly doctor who knew a lot more about my past than did Pauline. The next evening Pauline confirmed my fears. "Dr. Huffman was pretty stern about it, Jay," she said gently. "He told me you were a poor risk for a husband."

My chin sank to my chest. Tears filled my eyes. I couldn't speak. Suddenly she was in my arms, weeping too. "Oh, Jay! I do care for you very much. In some ways I wish I didn't. But please don't rush things."

That Saturday night I arranged for us to double date with an actress friend and her boyfriend. Susan, a buxom 30-year-old, had once had a crush on me before my capitulation to drugs. I thought it might help if Pauline found I was attractive to other women. I was hardly prepared for the explosion that took place.

We went to a movie, then returned to my hotel apartment where I had room service bring up bacon and eggs for the four of us. Susan had simpered and fawned over me all evening. Pauline was very quiet. When we entered my small, rather drab suite, Pauline looked it over with great curiosity. I had invited her up before, but she wouldn't come, which had made me respect her even more.

I saw Pauline stop and stare at the framed picture of Caligula

I had managed to salvage from the wreckage of my life. Then she went to my small kitchenette to help set things up for the eggs and bacon.

I sat down in an arm chair. In her high theatrical voice Susan began talking about my great impact on Hollywood. Then she came over and began stroking my head. "Jay, it's so good to see you again. It's been *such* a long time."

The door buzzer sounded and I bounced up to answer it, relieved to interrupt an awkward moment.

It was the waiter with our order. Soon we were seated at the small table, eagerly devouring this late evening meal. Except for Susan. She was not hungry and only picked at her food while dominating the conversation which, unfortunately for me and her date, centered on me.

When my plate was clean I moved back to the more comfortable arm chair. So did Susan. This time she came over, sat her ample self down in my lap and put her arms around me.

Pauline now came to life. She arose from the table, picked up Susan's uneaten plate of fried eggs and headed for us in the arm chair. "Susan," she said sweetly, "you didn't eat your eggs. But I really think Jay wants them."

With that she turned to me and with a deft flip of her hand tossed the eggs in my face.

I sat there stunned for a moment, delicate egg whites decorating my hair and deep rich yellow yokes running down my face onto my shirt and suit.

Susan shot out of my lap as though propelled from a gun and took refuge by her date.

Pauline stared at me calmly for a moment, laid the now empty plate on the table and tossed me a dish towel to clean up. Susan and her date decided it was time to leave.

I was seeing a totally new side of sweet, warm-hearted Pauline. As soon as the others had departed, she turned her attention to the picture of me as Caligula. I think she intended to fold it in two and throw it in the trash. Glass does not fold, however, and there were loud cracking noises as showers of broken glass splattered onto the floor.

Then she turned to me, a bit hysterically, I thought. "I hate this picture! I hate this role you played. It represents all the wrong things." Her eyes flashed.

Pauline picked up her purse and started to leave, but I grabbed her. "Now wait a minute. I'm going with you to your car. But let me clean up a bit first."

She looked at me carefully with those wide, brown eyes. This time there was steel in them, plus flecks of anger. "There's no need to do that," she said.

"Oh yes there is," I said, wiping yolk out of my eye. "My future wife is not about to go out walking alone at night in Hollywood, even if she can be as fierce as a wildcat."

Gradually I worked the smile back into her eyes. Suddenly she laughed. "Jay, as long as I live I'll never forget how you looked with egg all over your face."

The egg-throwing incident in my apartment convinced me of one thing: Pauline loved me. I continued to pursue her passionately and persistently. She asked me one night if I would take her to church.

"Sure," I said. "Which one?"

She named one on Sunset Boulevard. To my surprise she suggested we go on a Saturday afternoon when no one was there. I asked her why.

"I like to sit in an empty church and pray."

As we sat in a very quiet sanctuary, I looked up into the giant oaken beams and memories flooded back of my early life. Grandmother had prayed and gone to church, but the Lord let her die a painful death. God to me was a stern judge up there somewhere, if He existed at all. Pauline sat beside me, eyes closed, peaceful, serene. I envied her.

Later as we walked slowly down the boulevard, Pauline was silent. I opened the conversation.

"You haven't told me much about your religion, Pauline. Is it important to you?"

"I grew up hearing too many religious discussions," she said slowly. "Except for Mother, it seemed mostly talk. I guess I've become one of those people who try to walk it, not talk it."

"My grandmother was a Christian," I said. "She read the Bible to me, but I never understood it. I tried praying, but nothing ever happened."

"What did you pray for?"

"I prayed for my grandmother to get well. But she died." Tears filled my eyes. It still hurt to talk about it.

Pauline took my arm and squeezed it. "Deep down in you is a tender heart, Jay. That's what made me fall in love with you." I stopped suddenly on the sidewalk. The traffic noise seemed far away. She said she loved me! I melted inside. I started to say something; however, Pauline continued. "But there's a dark side to you, Jay, that scares me. I'm not sure I know how to deal with it."

I tried to reassure her. "Your love has brought out my good qualities, Pauline. Since meeting you I've come back to life. It was as though you turned on a light inside me. I feel I just can't go on living without you."

She was silent, her face troubled. "That kind of talk scares me, Jay. I can't be God in your life."

"You can show me the way."

"I don't know. I just don't know."

12

Comeback Begun

OUR CONVERSATION continued far into the night. We had driven up to Mulholland Drive in her Ford and sat looking out over the lights of Los Angeles spread beneath us like millions of diamonds some giant had cast onto endless black velvet.

"Some of the kids would make fun of me," mused Pauline, as she talked about her childhood in her hometown of Ada. "I never could resist nursing some wounded bird or animal," she said. Then she described how some sixth sense for the inaudible cry of pain brought her unerringly to the wounded bird lying under a bush, the sick cat curled up under the porch, the whimpering puppy behind the woodshed. If the animal died despite her ministrations, Pauline rounded up members of her family and friends to give the animal a proper funeral.

As she grew older, she was drawn to fellow human beings in trouble. Teen-agers alienated from parents sought her out. Lonely adults, especially older folks, gravitated toward her warm personality.

"I guess it was inevitable that I go into nursing," she mused. "But there were some people I couldn't help, particularly the two I loved very much."

Pauline's father and mother separated while she was still in grade school. "Dad had a problem with alcohol," she said. Pauline, her older sister Margaret, and her mother, Naomi Flowers, then moved to California. Margaret soon married and settled with her husband in Santa Ana. Pauline finished high school, took a job and was soon self-supporting. Pauline's father remained in Oklahoma to cope with declining health and alcoholism.

As Pauline told her story, I could tell how deeply my own terrible need had touched her. And there in the car that cool night high above the city, I asked her again to marry me.

She sat silent for a long time.

"I don't know, Jay," she said pensively. "I don't know."

I knew what she was thinking. Dr. Huffman had stated that I was a bad risk. Pauline already knew how an alcohol problem could destroy a marriage. And she sensed how very vulnerable I was.

But I believe this very vulnerability and openness is what stopped her from breaking off our romance altogether. For though she was as lonely as I was, she had been turned off by the slick, predatory Hollywood males. When I appeared in her office, I was like one of the wounded animals to which she had ministered as a child. My need was total.

Though she responded to my need, Pauline still wasn't sure that marriage would be right for both of us. As I pressed her for a "yes" answer, she hesitated, wanting to talk with her sister and mother about it but unwilling to do so. There was one Person to whom she could go, she said.

Pauline asked me to accompany her the next day to the same small church on Sunset Boulevard where we had gone before. Again we were the only ones there. And again, Pauline prayed quietly for some time while I studied the roof beams, hoping she'd be led to a favorable answer.

Finally, she indicated she was ready to go and I could hardly contain myself. Just outside the church doors, she stopped me on the sidewalk and took both my hands.

Her eyes were shining and she whispered: "Yes, Jay, yes."

I was jubilant.

Before getting married, we tallied up our financial assets; they were pitiful. My father had left a small insurance policy for me which provided $200 a month for five years. That had been my only source of income for many weeks. A final effort to get something out of my Bel Air house had failed. The papers I had signed for a third mortgage while wiped out on drugs drained my last bit of equity.

Pauline had her two-door coupe which was barely operable, plus a small savings account. We used most of her savings to pay my apartment-hotel bill. Then on February 8, 1960, we drove to Tijuana, Mexico, in her old car for a Mexican civil marriage ceremony. Hand in hand we walked through drab, pictureless halls to a crowded, stuffy room where a bored bureaucrat had us fill out several forms. In another dismal office an equally disinterested official read us the marriage ceremony. It took all of five minutes.

On the drive back to Hollywood, we were singing and laughing and sneaking kisses every time we stopped at a light. Just north of San Diego the Ford, overtaxed and overextended, blew a rod. A mechanic examined it and shook his head.

Sadly we pushed the forlorn little car off the road. Pauline looked so mournful I thought for a moment she was going to suggest we give it a proper funeral. The mechanic agreed to perform the burial act and took us to the nearest bus station.

We moved into a small $30-a-week apartment in Hollywood, only half a block from Grauman's Chinese Theatre where four of my movies had played. In fact, the long lines of people waiting to see *The Robe* had passed directly in front of our apartment entrance. The memories made me uneasy, but the apartment's reasonable rent, the fact that it was furnished and that I didn't have to sign a lease helped us make the choice. Since we had no car, it was necessary for us to live within walking distance of stores and Pauline's place of work.

Despite having so little money, the first months after our marriage were very happy ones. Hand in hand, like a couple of kids, we would window shop along Hollywood Boulevard, oblivious to everything around us.

With Pauline's help I was making progress in my rehabilitation. The wracking pains and intense suffering were over, but Pauline had to massage my back and legs regularly to combat the aches which persisted for some time. Some nights I awoke screaming, the horrible places I had been and the things I had done flashing through my brain. Pauline would soothe my troubled spirit with gentle words and soon I was able to go back to sleep.

Several times she suggested we attend services at a small interdenominational chapel nearby. These were my very first visits to any church service. I went because I knew it was what Pauline wanted. My estrangement from God was complete. To me, He was capricious and undependable. Pauline never tried to push her beliefs onto me. She also hesitated to tell her family of our marriage, waiting for just the right time, she told me.

As my thirtieth birthday approached I began to feel an onslaught of panic. I had vowed that by 30 I would play *Hamlet* on Broadway. Instead I had almost destroyed myself. No producer would give me work. My last film role had been almost three years before in *My Man Godfrey*. And I still had the possibility of a jail sentence hanging over me.

Pauline redoubled her ministry to me, pouring out love and support. "You haven't even begun to learn to live yet," she told me. "You've lived in a make-believe world so long that you don't know what real life is all about."

Torn by my emotional upsets, Pauline resigned her job with Dr. Huffman to give full time to our marriage. In order to economize, we moved to an even smaller and cheaper apartment. There was now only my $200-a-month insurance income. Once the electricity was turned off for nonpayment of the bill; I remember one meal when we had nothing but a solitary baked potato between us.

Then came a joyous moment. I picked up a copy of the *Los Angeles Times* at the newsstand and was skimming through its pages when, in the back of the paper, a tiny article caught my eye. The headline read: "Actor's Dope Conviction Reversed by Appellate Court." Reading on with mounting excitement I learned that judicial errors had been discovered in my case. Only too well did I recall the harshness of that judge and the peremptory manner in which he had remanded me to that terrifying jail.

A feeling of euphoria washed over me. I ran back to the apartment, brandishing the newspaper, tears in my eyes. "Read this! Read this!" I shouted.

Pauline did so, then broke down and sobbed. "Does this mean that you're completely cleared?" she asked uncertainly.

"Of course."

"But why didn't your lawyer contact you instead of having to read it in the newspapers," she asked.

"I don't know and don't care. I'm sure that I'll get some kind of letter about it pretty soon."

But no letter came.

Then came another turn in our fortunes. Concerned about our situation, Vega Maddux, an old friend, urged us to move to the ocean where she felt the fresh sea air would help heal me. Vega, a buxom opera singer who had appeared on the Jimmy Durante show doing comedy and singing, knew a writer who had a house close to the beach in Venice, California.

Though it was a lovely spot, the population of Venice included many aged and impoverished people scratching out their retirement years on Social Security, intermixed with a sprinkling of addicts, drunks, muggers, drug pushers and beatniks.

However, when Vega's friend offered to rent us a furnished room for $40 a month, we quickly agreed, sight unseen. Carrying our belongings in suitcases, we took a bus out to Venice and hunted the address we'd been given. Our landlord took us to the room and vanished.

For several minutes Pauline and I stood in the middle of it, unable to say anything. It was a tiny room with a kitchenette. There were two rickety chairs and one single bed only thirty inches wide. We looked at each other with the unspoken question hanging between us: How could we live in this?

Pauline walked to the window and lifted it. A fresh sea breeze ruffled the frayed curtain and she turned to me and smiled. "It's all right, Jay, we can manage."

We slept in the little bed curled up closely like two spoons in a drawer. But Vega was right; the air was good and the atmosphere relaxing.

Now married four months, we found ourselves subsisting mainly on peanut butter sandwiches. Then Pauline told me one evening that she was pregnant. I was overjoyed! Then I began to worry. Being so short of money, how could we pay a doctor? And peanut butter was hardly the right diet for an expectant mother. Meanwhile, as she increased in girth, our bed seemed to become smaller and smaller.

It was at this point that Pauline decided to tell her parents and sister about our marriage, how happy we had been for the past four months and how much we were looking forward to our first child. Meanwhile, Pauline and I were inseparable; we went everywhere together exploring the little streets and the beach area. Among the forlorn bingo parlors and fortune-teller establishments, was a small twenty-five-seat storefront theatre.

When the proprietor learned that I was an actor, he asked for my help. Although he couldn't pay me, it felt good to be performing before an audience again. I did readings from the classics, Shakespeare, Poe, and Kipling. We even put an ad in the Santa Monica newspaper about my appearances in this theatre, located only six blocks from the courthouse where my trial had been held.

One of the people who seemed to enjoy listening to my renditions was a neighbor, a beachfront character everybody called "Little Lottie." Lottie had played the piano in the silent movie houses, but when talking pictures came in Little Lottie went out. She was a tiny butterball of a woman with a little girl's voice that sounded like Betty Boop, and a head of frizzy curls that made her look like a septuagenarian "Little Orphan Annie." Irrepressibly good-humored and kindhearted, she decided to adopt us.

There was the time when my monthly insurance check was stolen from our mailbox—a major crisis. I told Pauline that we now had no money to buy food. Pauline began praying. In disgust I turned to the window and looked out on the mean little streets, berating life for the way it had treated us.

When Little Lottie found out about our plight, she said, "Don't worry, kids." Each day she would show up with fresh fruits, vegetables and other footstuffs.

"Enjoy it," was all she would say.

When we protested that she couldn't afford to give us food like this, she would shrug it off and show up the next day with more bounty.

Not only was this a reprieve from near starvation, her fare was much more tasty than peanut butter sandwiches.

Then one day we discovered how she was getting the food. Lottie foraged through the garbage cans of local supermarkets and restaurants. She would retrieve, for example, a head of wilted lettuce from the muck, pluck off the outside brown leaves and it would be as good as new—almost. Among a rotten bunch of bananas would be a few good ones. It was also amazing how much good food the restaurants tossed out.

Not caring to be choosy, we continued eating, courtesy of Little Lottie's enterprise.

Lottie also patrolled the beach looking for dropped coins and other riches, like a geologist searching for oil. Sometimes she made a strike. If so, she would share with us what little goodies she had found.

Pauline and I would occasionally join Little Lottie in far-ranging expeditions for buried treasure. Our booty: soft drink bottles which we could turn in for two cents each. I learned much from Lottie about life, especially how the poor must scratch daily for mere existence. Meanwhile, Pauline was able to find a part-time job bottling salad dressing in a shabby warehouse nearby.

When acquaintances moved out of a garage apartment further down the beach, we moved in because it contained a larger bed. It was a little like a crow's nest, but it would do. Now we could get more sleep.

My lifelong love affair with monkeys resulted in my acquiring one from an old Italian organ grinder on the beach. He was a small capuchin, 25 years old, who could no longer work the streets with his master. With a wispy, scraggly beard, he answered to the name of Beardsley.

When I was at home, Beardsley was a model of well-mannered decorum. But when I was gone, Pauline complained that he wrecked the place. That was hard for me to believe, so Pauline suggested I bid a loud farewell, tiptoe back in and surprise him.

I did, caught Beardsley misbehaving and spanked him. He took his revenge by biting Pauline's wrist clear through to the bone with his dirty quarter-century-old yellow teeth. Beardsley had to go.

With our baby nearly due, I began frantically searching for any kind of job. One day an ad in the paper caught my attention; a man was wanted to care for the young animals in the Lynwood Baby Zoo. I was not only hired for $75 a week, but the zoo also agreed to take Beardsley.

I was soon working twelve hours a day, six days a week in animal stench and filth. But I loved those animals and was strangely content. In addition to monkeys, I looked after baby lions, tigers and elephants. I even had an opportunity to train some of the chimps into a fairly decent comedy act.

By now we had moved into a much nicer apartment in Lynwood close to the zoo and Pauline was happy with a flower-filled garden complete with orange trees. After our days as beachcombers at Venice this was a real step upward. With our rent only $65 a month we were eating better than at any time in our marriage and Pauline was able to have medical care.

When Pauline went into the hospital to give birth, I was the complete caricature of the nervous, distraught father-to-be. I stayed with her in the labor room, shared her pain with moans and grimaces, held her hand tightly. When the hospital staff tried to get me to leave the room, I refused to go. When they took her to the delivery room, I searched out the chaplain and prevailed upon him to go up and see how Pauline was doing.

The chaplain soon returned with the good news that at 6:59 P.M. our son had been born. The date was February 28, 1961. The new baby weighed in at six pounds, fifteen ounces. We named him Jay Paul.

When we took him home, we had no crib; so we made one from an empty cardboard box picked up at the supermarket. As we had no layette, Pauline's mother, Naomi, and sister, Margaret, put together the things needed for a baby. Later they gave us both a used crib and bassinette. We felt like millionaires when we took Jay Paul out of the box and installed him in his own crib.

With my outdoor work at the zoo, I was building up my body

and regaining my health. I had already celebrated my first anniversary free of drugs. For the first time we could save a little money. Pauline insisted upon it. "You're not an animal-cage cleaner, Jay. You're an actor and you must go back to your profession. If you can't get parts here, let's go back East where you can work in plays."

We finally decided that as soon as we had saved enough money to buy a good used car, we would head East. Deep down I was fearful. Despite the hardships and poverty of eighteen months of married life, I had never been happier. For the first time there was meaning to life. I loved and was loved. We had produced a wonderful child. My bodily health was almost completely restored. Unable to give thanks to a Father God, I transferred it to Pauline whom I felt had made it all possible, not realizing that this is one way to destroy the one you love so much.

13

Journey to the Past

IT WAS MY MARRIAGE to Pauline that started me on my comeback.
For the first eighteen months we lived in California. For numerous
reasons we shouldn't have left that state. Pauline did not want to
go, but she felt the only way I could regain my self-respect was
to start over, away from the bad memories and bad associations
in the Los Angeles area. I had no inner guidance system that could
have helped.

The situation came to a head one evening when a neighbor dropped in to say that *The Robe* and *Demetrius and the Gladiators*
were playing as a double feature in a nearby theatre. "Would you
like to go?" I asked Pauline since she had not seen either film.

"No!" she answered.

"Why not?" I asked somewhat hurt.

Pauline's brown eyes flashed little sparks which I first recognized
the night she threw a plate of eggs at me. "That role of the mad
emperor was bad for you, Jay."

Her attitude seemed completely unreasonable. "But it's only a
part I played. The *New York Times* said it was one of the ten
best performances in the history of films."

"I know all about that, Jay. But it became more than a role
for you. You lived the part. It almost destroyed you."

"But Boris Karloff played some horrible roles in films and I
never met a kinder man in my whole life."

"Karloff left those roles in the studio when he went home each day. You took Caligula with you."

"So that's why you hate the picture so much. You're jealous."

Pauline had shattered the glass in the picture frame of Caligula that night of the egg throwing, but I had rescued the picture before she destroyed it. I would put it in a prominent place; Pauline would move it to a dark corner.

"Listen to me, Jay," she said earnestly. "I want you to build a new life for yourself and for Jay Paul and me. Of course I'm jealous of Caligula or anyone who would take you from your family. He's a threat to me."

I took her in my arms suddenly overwhelmed by my good fortune to have a wife who truly loved me and who had put light into my life. But I didn't get rid of the picture.

Several weeks later we bought a six-year-old Buick that seemed in good condition. We gave up our apartment, got rid of everything we couldn't pack in the car and fixed up a bed of pillows in the back seat for Jay Paul. Our destination was Miami Beach where I felt some old friends could help me revive my acting career. It was a foolish adventure. We had less than $100 to cover meals and gas for a trip by car across the entire country.

Several days before we were to leave, Pauline called her mother in Santa Ana to make arrangements to stop there on our way to Florida. When she hung up the phone, a thought struck her. "Is there someone you should contact about leaving Los Angeles—I mean about your court case?"

"But my conviction has been overturned by the court."

"I know that. But will they need you here for anything?"

"I don't see why. I haven't heard a word from them for more than two years."

"Should you let your lawyer know where you're going?" Pauline persisted.

"That's a good idea. I'll drop him a note."

An interruption wiped the thought from my mind. It didn't seem important. Just one small thing left undone. Like most citizens, I found court procedures bewildering and formidable. Anyway, the news story about my exoneration by the court seemed final and

official. Yet what a difference a call to my lawyer at that point
would have made!

During our visit with Pauline's mother, Naomi, Jay Paul was
the center of attention. How quickly a small baby can bring together
a family of different backgrounds and beliefs! For the first time I
felt that Naomi had a degree of confidence in me. "I'll be praying
for you, Jay," she told me. "And I believe you'll find the answers
to all your needs."

After we drove on, everything went smoothly until we hit a violent
rainstorm in mountain passes outside of Phoenix. We then discovered that our wiper blades were so old the windshield was a blur
from the torrents of rain. Driving was treacherous, especially on
mountain roads that twisted and turned in serpentine coils with
sheer drops into rocky canyons.

Ahead of us loomed the lights of a gas station and we turned
into it with a feeling of gratitude. New blades were put on. I asked,
"How much?"

"Twenty-five dollars," came the reply.

We stared at the man in amazed horror. He was adamant.

"I know I'm overcharging you," he said calmly, "but you've
got to have them."

I pleaded with him. "We're driving all the way across the country
and have very little money."

"That's your problem, Mister," he said. "If you want the blades,
that's my price."

I stared forlornly at the downpour, angrily paid the $25 and
we continued our journey. After a motel stop that first night, our
funds were already half gone.

Our next stop was in Ada, Oklahoma, where Pauline had been
born. Ada was a charmingly small rural college town, with streets
shaded by overhanging trees. Lawns were green and neatly kept;
a sense of peace surrounded us as we drove into the city limits.

Fletcher Flowers, Pauline's father, turned out to be a tall, lanky,
Lincolnesque man with green eyes who looked a lot like Henry
Fonda. He had been a shoemaker until his retirement. His black
hair now had a sprinkling of grey, and he was quietly humorous.
We learned that he had overcome his drinking problem.

The family was more like a clan and the men in the family seemed

to be all pastors, lay preachers, deacons or elders. They staged a
country church picnic in our honor. Pauline and I boggled at the
grapefruit-sized red tomatoes, the piles of crunchy fried chicken,
great slabs of orange-red hams, yellow corn on the cob, green beans,
and bowls of fruit. Country fiddlers took over after dinner and
young and old were soon square dancing on the grass. We were
certainly far from Hollywood.

Jay Paul was again the center of attention and Pauline and I
both felt as if we had been clasped to the bosom of the family.
This was a very unusual feeling for me. I had never enjoyed a
real family and saw it here for the first time. Though turned off
by the religious jargon, I absorbed their love like a thirsty plant.

When we left, Pauline's father pressed enough money on us for
the balance of the trip, then clasped me in his arms. With tears
in his eyes, he said, "You take good care of my daughter and grand-
child."

The rest of the trip was uneventful. As we drove into Florida,
I began to see the old familiar landmarks of my childhood. We
had no sooner settled in an apartment motel when the phone rang.
Pauline picked it up; from what she said I could tell it was from
her sister. Then her face became clouded. She listened further, then
hung up the receiver.

"Jay," she said quietly, "they just got word that your mother
has passed away. It happened while we were on the road. The
funeral was held two days ago."

For a few moments I was numbed. Then the tears came. Along
with the agony of losing my mother, waves of guilt and remorse
washed over me. I had been too self-centered to help a mother
who didn't know how to relate to her son. I found myself mourning
for the lost love neither of us knew how to give the other. Now
it was too late.

Her estate was so small that it could all be handled over the
telephone and by correspondence.

To launch my career in south Florida, I carefully composed a
letter to George Bourke, then entertainment editor for the *Miami
Herald* and an old friend. George ran the letter in its entirety in

his column, together with my photograph. It was through this that
I met Ruth Foreman who was running the Studio M Playhouse
in Coral Gables. Together we went over a group of plays in which
I might perform. The Nobel prize-winning French playwright, Albert Camus, had written one that seemed perfect. It was *Caligula*—
a stage dramatization of my famous movie part.

That night I told Pauline that I not only had found work in a
local theatre, but that I was starring in the next play.

"That's wonderful, Jay," she said. "What is the play?"

Suddenly I found myself hesitating. "It's by that great French
existentialist writer, Albert Camus."

"Yes."

"The title may surprise you. It's *Caligula.*"

"Jay! Not again!" Pauline's dismay annoyed me.

"This is a stage production. A lot different from the movies I
did."

"Jay, it's the same story, isn't it?"

"Well, yes."

"That role brings you nothing but grief."

"Not this time. I'll do like Boris Karloff did and leave it in the
theatre when I finish. It's different now because I have you and
Jay Paul to come home to."

"I still don't like it."

"We have got to eat and this will pay me five hundred dollars
a week," I said firmly.

The press coverage began and it was all favorable. Everywhere
I went my name was in print: in the social columns, on the drama
page, in the amusement ads. When we began rehearsals, Pauline
helped sew costumes for the cast and we were both busily occupied
for the first time in our marriage. Pauline's opposition to the choice
of the play subsided.

Caligula opened on January 15, 1962, for an eight-week run.
We sold out for every performance. The notices were wonderful:
"Cries of 'Bravo' greeted Jay Robinson . . . Robinson is marvelously
mad . . . always powerful, moving."

When these reviews hit we were clasped to the bosom of Miami
society. Invitations came to every kind of party: in lavish homes,

hotel ballrooms and aboard yachts cruising Miami waters. Caligula had come home in triumphant style. How wrong Pauline had been!

As I left the theatre one evening, I noticed someone lurking in the shadows. It was Pat, the girl who had lured me to the resort motel where I had been robbed and beaten. She was haggard, worn and spiritless. Only 35, she looked 50. Why seek me out at this particular time? I wondered. She could not go back to California, she said tearfully. There was still a warrant out for her arrest there. If I signed the paper she had with her, absolving her of complicity in the robbery, she could return.

For an instant I hesitated. The painful memory of the beating her boyfriend had given me and losing the $3,400 shot anger through me. I was about to turn away when something stopped me. I actually found myself feeling sorry for her. I signed the paper and she disappeared into the night.

After *Caligula* I starred in two more plays at Studio M, each less successful at the box office than the one before it. I played *Hamlet* with the Miami University student performers, and then did a one-man show at the Coconut Grove Playhouse which included three versions of Caligula in the final scene of the show: Caligula in *The Robe,* in the stage play *Caligula,* by Albert Camus, and a Caligula scene from *Lazarus Laughed,* a play by Eugene O'Neill. I gave performances for numerous church and civic groups in the area.

And so passed 1962, starting with a triumph and gradually winding down as the year progressed. I started at $500 a week, went to $250, and by the turn of the new year, I was lucky if I could earn $100 a week. And I had many weeks without salary at all. It was as if my success as Caligula had tainted everything that followed.

As my appearances on stage declined, so did our invitations to parties. The pattern was the same as before, a microcosm of my Hollywood experience—with one big difference. I now had Pauline and Jay Paul behind me to add their strength to mine and I no longer had to retreat from reality. Pauline did not remind me of her fears about the Caligula role and I didn't care to think about it.

But I needed work if we were to eat. The $200-a-month income from my father's insurance had run out. The answer was a new kind of role in "The Monkey Jungle."

In 1932, Joseph Dumond, a college professor, and his wife, Grace, bought ten acres of cheap hammock land at $10 an acre south of Miami. It was almost virgin jungle. Next he purchased twelve Java monkeys of both sexes for $10 apiece. His total outlay initially was $220. He then conducted a rather unique experiment by turning the monkeys loose in this jungle to see if they would colonize it.

The area was very similar in climate and appearance to the jungles of their native land and it quickly became a monkey's Eden. It became unique in another way too. The monkeys run free; the humans are in cages. A screened walkway meanders through the jungle, inside of which are the human sightseers, peering at the monkeys outside. People were flocking to it in huge numbers, and it was well on its way to becoming a major tourist attraction.

Because of my interest in monkeys as a kid in Florida, the Dumonds remembered me and had followed my film career in Hollywood. When I explained my need, they were only too glad to give me a job at $100 a week. I was hired as a tour guide and soon developed quite a spiel.

The park was managed by the Dumonds' son, Frank, who was very good to me. Yet I still suffered a hard root of insecurity deep inside. When I heard that Frank's wife was unhappy with the added cost of an extra tour guide, it bothered me. Suddenly afraid I might lose my job, I regressed in age twelve years to my Broadway-type deceptions. At the end of each tour, I would go to the rest room. Inside my pockets I carried assorted pens and pencils. In the privacy of one of the cubicles, I would fill in visitors' comment cards with carefully contrasting styles of handwriting.

"Your tour guide was wonderful," I wrote on one card. "Mr. Robinson was very entertaining," I put on another. When no one was looking, I would slip a dozen or more such cards into the box placed at the exit for "customer comments." I never was asked why I had to go to the rest room so often and the cards seemed to impress the Dumonds.

But after almost two years in Miami, it was time to move on. We weren't making it on my salary at the Monkey Jungle and my employment potential on the Miami theatre scene had been exhausted.

Twelve years had passed since I had last acted on Broadway. Now I felt the time had come to assault its heights once again.

We drove out of Miami, the old Buick crammed with everything we owned in the world, looking like Baghdad bazaar merchants on their way to market. We had no view at all out of the rear window and the eight-year-old car sputtered along on its threadbare tires like an elderly asthmatic.

Jay Paul was installed in a baby seat between Pauline and me. To conserve our tiny capital we ate only the cheapest of food and stopped overnight in any rickety motel if the price was low enough.

The blowout came just as we were approaching Philadelphia. I had never changed a tire before and wrestled valiantly with rusted, frozen lugs and a tire wrench. Classical actors can spout long, silken sentences, but they are usually helpless with tools and everyday tasks. Somehow I got the spare on, but our tire situation was now desperate. With only $40 left we couldn't afford new ones.

It was then we sighted a junkyard piled high with old tires, batteries and spare parts. We bought two used tires there for three dollars each.

Strangely enough, the man putting the tires on for us recognized me. "Aren't you Jay Robinson?" he inquired. "I saw you in *The Robe*. What are you doing here in Philadelphia?"

When I explained our destination and goal, he got excited. "There's a wealthy dentist here who's a patron of the arts. I'm sure he'd sponsor a play for you," he enthused.

A call to the doctor brought an invitation to visit him at his home. The doctor's house was beautiful—three stories of gleaming fresh paintwork set amid immaculately tended lawns and surrounded by wrought iron railings. A brass plate proclaimed: "Dr. L. Grant, D.D.S."

When our battered Buick pulled up in front of this palatial mansion, it was like the Beverly Hillbillies arriving in the Hills of Beverly.

All three of us were covered with a thick layer of grime from the long trip north. Our car was stuffed full of personal possessions, including a big bag of dirty diapers.

We walked into the doctor's reception room and announced ourselves. The attractive black nurse, in a crisp, starched uniform, regarded us from under raised eyebrows. We could see the words revolving inside her head. *This is a famous actor?*

Dr. Grant came out to welcome us. He was a portly, distinguished man who looked like a black James Bond. His large, handsome face glistened above his white dental coat. "I saw you in *The Robe,* Mr. Robinson. Magnificent performance." We shook hands warmly.

When he found out I had played *Caligula* to record-breaking crowds in Florida, he was more than pleased. "You can stay here with us," he invited.

We were shown to a suite of rooms on the top floor of the house. Dr. Grant didn't know it, but this was the most comfortable home Pauline and I had enjoyed since our marriage.

He had an ample staff of servants, including the nurse, a maid and a cook. We were invited to dine with the Grants and were flabbergasted at the opulence. A crystal chandelier sprinkled diamonds of light over pure white napery and was in turn reflected up again from sterling silver and gleaming bone china. The maid served a lavish dinner of piping hot soul food.

Mrs. Grant was not only a brilliant woman and a biologist, she was also beautiful with red hair and a light coffee-colored skin. She looked like some glamorous South American hostess.

And here we were, poor whites enjoying the bounty. The house was run like some gracious southern mansion, only the plantation owner was black.

We discussed putting on *Caligula* but insurmountable union problems caused us to settle on a one-man show to be climaxed by a *Caligula* scene. Pauline was unhappy about it. "Something always goes wrong when you play that role," she said.

"Nonsense," I replied.

On the night of the performance, like a couple of white Cinderellas in rented tux and gown, Pauline and I swept through the darkened evening streets of Philadelphia in our pumpkin coach—a gleaming, block-long limousine, rented for the occasion, complete with chauffer.

We entered the ballroom and found ourselves surrounded by a multitude of cheerful, happy black faces. My performance was received with polite applause until the long *Caligula* speech at the end. The audience nearly split open the roof with their response.

After the show, Pauline and I went back to the Grant residence where a champagne after-the-show party was in progress. I had purified my system so completely that only two drinks went right to my head. I remember stumbling upstairs with much assistance from Pauline. I don't remember much more until I awoke suddenly, gasping for air, to find our room full of smoke.

I looked around frantically for its cause, which wasn't hard to find. I had apparently fallen asleep smoking a cigarette. It had ignited the mattress.

Pulling Pauline and Jay Paul out of the way, I dragged the mattress over to a window and threw it out onto Dr. Grant's immaculate lawn where it lay, gently smouldering.

We slept the rest of the night on the floor.

The next morning I was groggily gazing out the window when the dignified Dr. Grant walked by, apparently admiring his lush green lawn. Instead, he viewed a sour-smelling, very charred wreck of one of his mattresses. Then he looked up and saw me. We stared hesitantly at each other for a long moment; I grinned weakly and waved.

Our good-bys were a bit strained, but as we climbed into our Buick, Pauline had in her hand a check for $500 as payment for one night's work. "You may not want me to play Caligula," I said loftily, "but it sure pays well."

Pauline's usually serene face was clouded. "It could have been a good experience, but somehow it wasn't. You drank too much last night, we ruined their mattress and I somehow don't feel right about taking this check."

On our way to New York City, we cashed the check, and then stopped at a supermarket in New Jersey to buy a few supplies. Jay Paul was asleep in the front seat and I was lying down in the back still groggy from my celebration the night before. I heard

Pauline climb back into the car. I opened my eyes. Instead of Pauline, a strange man was in the front seat.

"What are you doing?" I croaked, sitting up.

The man jerked around, surprised to see someone pop up in the back seat. An apologetic look replaced surprise on his face. "I'm sorry, sir," he said. "I have the same make and model car; I must have made a mistake."

With that he climbed out and disappeared. Pauline returned shortly and I'm sure her cries could have been heard in Miami. "Where's my purse?"

The man who had been in our front seat had taken it. With it had gone most of our $500. Pauline had taken $20 into the supermarket. All we had now to face Broadway was a half a tank of gas and the change left from her shopping.

14

Broadway Revisited

WE ENTERED NEW YORK City late in the summer of 1963 with a blind and naive optimism. First, a car is more a liability than an asset in New York; we did not even possess the financial means to park it safely. Our identification and driver's licenses had been looted from us by the robber in New Jersey. In fast succession we dismissed several possibilities such as to phone Pauline's family in California or Oklahoma for help, and to deliver ourselves to the tender mercy of the New York Traveler's Aid Society.

We were armed with one telephone number—that of the Greenwich Village apartment of a producer I knew, Andy Milligan. I had called him from Philadelphia for technical help when I first thought the *Caligula* play would be produced by the Grants. He had leased a small ninety-nine seat theatre called the Showboat where he produced off-Broadway shows. He told me to look him up when we got to New York.

The Showboat was a theatre-in-the-round, located at Second Avenue and Fourteenth Street. Andy was interested in presenting a play based upon the Oscar Wilde novel, *The Picture of Dorian Gray.* Would I consider the starring role of Lord Henry Wotton? Of course I would. Then Andy came up with a place for us to stay during the initial run of the play.

Andy had a friend whose elderly mother was out of New York for a few weeks and we were welcome to use her empty apartment in Brooklyn. I told him this would do nicely.

Temperatures near 100 degrees boiled the city. Hazy waves of heat, tainted with blue motor exhaust, rose skyward from streets on which the asphalt was heated to a spongy black goo. As we drove through Manhattan and across the Brooklyn Bridge, we noticed that people walked very slowly, looking wilted and bedraggled. Kids were taking showers in spurting streams of lukewarm water from open fire hydrants. We were soaked with perspiration and gasping for breath.

The apartment was in the middle of Brooklyn's most ethnic Hassidic neighborhood of impoverished but very pious Jews. Men paraded in the heat with their long black locks, curly black beards, big floppy hats and enveloping black coats.

Our elderly landlady no doubt loved every inch of her apartment with its overstuffed and ancient furnishings. We, in turn, were very grateful to find a job and a free apartment on our first day in the city. But how we suffered.

The apartment was not just tiny, it was so full of beloved mementos, furniture and bric-a-brac that we hardly had room to turn around. When we opened the door, it was like peeking into an oven to see how the roast was doing. A blast of hot musty air seemed to sear us. The old lady, apparently fearful of thieves, had nailed the windows shut. Outside the apartment it was 102 degrees. Inside the tiny space it must have been 120.

This one-room apartment measured twelve feet square, had a small cupboard-sized kitchen, and a pullman bath. There was no way we could open a window short of breaking the glass. The radio did not work. The couch made up into a single bed. The one fan was so small it had absolutely no effect on the heavy overheated air that lay limp within the room like a waterlogged blanket.

All night we perspired, twisting, turning and gasping for air. Jay Paul was the only one to close his eyes for any length of time. But when the morning sun shone on his tiny pale face so beaded with sweat, I panicked. Was this truly all I could give my child?

The very next day I joined in the effort to assemble our cast and get "Dorian Gray" into rehearsal. I worked feverishly, for it was not only my comeback performance in New York, I was also to receive a percentage of the gross box-office receipts.

All day we labored at the Showboat. At night we returned to our "hot box" in Brooklyn. Pauline and I found our tempers flaring from lack of sleep. Then new blows fell. We noticed Jay Paul's glands were swollen and he was becoming fitful and crying a lot. He had the mumps.

I was in a new panic. Here I was a 33-year-old who had never had the mumps as a child and who had heard how dangerous they can be to an adult. I was rail thin now, down to about 128 pounds, resulting from long hours of work, sleepless nights in the "hot box" and poor food. I noticed that Pauline too had become thinner. The sparkle was gone from her eyes. She took care of Jay Paul automatically; I saw her on her knees a lot, praying, and this made me feel uncomfortable and inadequate. I wanted to succeed so that she and Jay Paul could have the comforts of life.

On the opening night of the play, only a small audience showed up. Although my personal reviews were good, the critics dismissed our effort saying, "It does not work as a play." It was a personal tragedy for Andy Milligan who had worked so hard to adapt the novel into a play.

During the nights that followed the opening our average audience numbered twenty-five. Some performances we played to as few as ten people. The play closed after three weeks.

Since I was out of work again, we had to find somewhere else to live. The friend's mother was returning soon. A rental agent got us a fourth floor walkup in a slum tenement building at 199 East Seventh Street in Manhattan. The rent was $87.50 a month.

Our new apartment not only was entirely empty of furniture, it did not have even a stove or refrigerator. We began to haunt the junk furniture stores of Second Avenue. For a stove we bought a two burner hotplate. An old bed we purchased was held together with bailing wire and would vibrate wildly with every movement we made. The mattress was old and stained but the cleanest we could find for the money. There was not enough money for carpeting so we lived on bare wooden boards.

The view out of our windows was of a decaying building about twelve feet across an alley. Dirty, begrimed brick, crumbling plaster and paint-chipped wooden window frames stared bleakly back at us. A sagging fire escape clung precariously to the wall of our building.

We left our window open until one night when a huge, cat-sized rat glared balefully at us from the steel parapet. Its fearless eyes struck terror. The window stayed closed after that through all kinds of weather.

There was a steel-covered door to our apartment, leading out into the hallway. The building supervisor advised us to keep the deadbolt on it locked at all times against prowlers and thieves.

When the weather turned cold, I was thankful for the wool suit that I had worn on stage as Lord Henry. Andy Milligan had let me keep it when the play folded. Otherwise our family had virtually no winter clothes. Everything had been bought earlier for the warmth of Florida. Our shoes were in such bad condition that we stuffed them with newspapers to cover the holes in the soles. Our feet now were constantly wet and cold.

Reluctantly I let Pauline take a job as a dental assistant. Disillusioned by the theatrical world, she told the dentist that her husband was a zookeeper. Since her job was across town Pauline had to use both bus and subway to get to work.

Christmas came and we did our best to make it a festive affair. Our most lavish investment was a $10 used tricycle for our little son, now 3, who, through all the hard times, had been good-tempered and undemanding. Jay Paul was delighted over this decrepit vehicle with its peeling paint and rusted chrome. My heart ached to see him so grateful for such a small gift.

Meanwhile I had been contacting all the agents, taking Jay Paul with me since Pauline was working. No one wanted me. My Hollywood drug reputation had scared them off.

Walking around the city, I continually found myself surrounded by cold, ruthless predators, men and women dazed by drugs or stumbling from alcoholism or drawn into themselves through fear or heartlessness.

One day a man fell to the sidewalk in the throes of what looked to be a heart attack. He was not a drunk. People just stepped over or around the body and kept going. I tried to lift his head from the damp, cold sidewalk. One person trod on my hand; another, not seeing me, knocked me right off my feet. I went inside and called an ambulance and waited until he was taken to the hospital.

On another occasion I saw two young thugs trying to break into the steel grilled front of a closed store. A man in front of me turned to his wife. "Look at those kids breaking into that store," he said.

"His wife was a typically philosophical New Yorker. "How do we know it's not their store?" she asked. They walked on.

I once saw an old man knocked down in a busy crowded street by several young hoods. Blood trickled down his face, blinding him. But he was tough. Instead of staying down and letting them take his money, the old guy kept getting up, holding onto his wallet with both hands and yelling. As fast as he got up, the thugs knocked him down again. The crowd edged around the scene, not interfering. By the time I reached a phone to call the police, the attackers has wrested the wallet loose and taken off.

Pauline learned the rules on how to survive in the modern concrete jungle: keep doors locked at all times, don't walk by yourself at night, and—most important of all—don't interfere in someone else's business.

One day I slipped on a broken sidewalk curbing and hurt my leg. It didn't seem serious, but the fall affected my joints and soon I couldn't walk. I was partially paralyzed. When this condition lasted some six to eight weeks, things became even more difficult for Pauline. Now she not only worked long hours but had both a small child and a husband to look after.

Although she was coughing constantly, Pauline had taken a second job at night to try to make ends meet. With her constant encouragement, I had recovered enough from my injury to begin again making the circuit of agents and theatrical offices. I still met with a stony rejection everywhere.

Finally, early in 1965, I landed a job with a bus and truck tour of 120 high schools in Connecticut and North Carolina. To provide both theatre and education, we were to stage such classics as *Julius Caesar* and *Twelfth Night* for the edification of high school students.

My salary of $200 a week made it possible for Pauline to quit her jobs and stay home to care for Jay Paul. While on tour I tried to phone her every night. Each time her voice sounded more and more husky. I prevailed on her to get a medical checkup.

A few days later when she answered the phone I could tell some-

thing was terribly wrong. At last I wrung it out of her. The test
results showed her to be in an advanced condition of pulmonary
tuberculosis.

I immediately rushed back to New York. Through my Screen
Actor's Guild membership, arrangements were made for Pauline
to enter the Will Rogers Memorial Hospital at Saranac Lake, New
York.

Our last night together before the hospital was heartrending. All
night I sat up, holding Pauline in my arms, comforting her as best
I could while a cold rain beat against the windows of the apartment.
I noticed that our little place was warm and comfortable; she had
managed to make it a home for us. My throat tightened and my
tears mingled with hers.

"Jay," she said softly, "we're not going to make it without God's
help." She looked up at me and placed a feverish hand on my
wet cheek. "I haven't pushed my beliefs on you, Dear. But we're
in deep trouble now. Seek Him while I'm gone, will you Jay? And
pray for me?"

Mutely I nodded. The next morning I took Pauline out to the
airport and put her on a small twin-engine plane bound for Saranac.
Then I stood with little Jay Paul at my side, in the chilly spring
wind, watching the emaciated white face of the person I loved most
in the world looking back at me through the cabin window. Her
usually lustrous brown eyes were so sunken they seemed like great
dark pits.

As I waved good-by, total grief overwhelmed me. Here was the
most loving, patient, selfless person I had ever known. For five
years she had given everything to our marriage. So many times we
had moved our home; she had accepted it without resentment. In
some miraculous way she had been a loving wife, a devoted mother
and often the breadwinner. Now it had broken her.

How could Pauline's God let this happen to her? I fumed as I
drove back into the city. How could I pray to a God who was so
heartless to those who loved Him?

15

Crisis at Saranac Lake

IF NEW YORK HAD been difficult for Pauline and me together, it became a place of impossible torment without her. The doctors had been so pessimistic that I was terrified she would never return. It further broke me up to see four-year-old Jay Paul look up from his rusting tricycle with troubled eyes and say, "Daddy, when will Mommy come home?"

As soon as she was settled in her room at Will Rogers Memorial Hospital, Pauline and I talked on the telephone. She was very reassuring: her room was comfortable, there was a lovely view, the nurses were considerate, the doctor cheerful, the food good, the other patients friendly. Knowing Pauline's gift of always thinking about others, I knew she was trying to bolster my spirits.

On April 14, my birthday, Pauline wrote me her first letter. Two days later I sat at the apartment window reading and rereading it.

Jay Darling: Please have a happy thirty-fifth birthday. From 29 to 35 you have blossomed into a most beautiful man. Imagine what 40 can be. I am so terribly proud of you—thanks, friend, pal, lover and *patient one.*

Dearest one, most of all on your birthday know how much I respect you—as a person, and for the abilities that God has given you. What can I say to start a brilliant light within you to create and to succeed? God allowed you to have this great gift. You must believe this.

129

And remember, Dear, I've prayed to God to restore you and to do with me as He sees fit. Don't you see, it is as if we are being tested? Thank you for five years of love and adoration.

From the beginning and all through the agonizing years of being together, Pauline had had the simple faith that it was the Lord who brought us together, that He had endowed me with wondrous gifts of talent, the better to fulfill His plan for me. She believed and prayed and I loved her for her faith. But I was grateful to her that she did not ask me to believe as she did. Now that she had asked me to pray, however, I tried. But I felt as if I were groping through a dark cloud.

My words were wooden. I remembered how I had once prayed that God would heal my grandmother. Instead she died. Whenever I had prayed desperately for something, it came back ashes. I could not pray with any fervor and conviction for Pauline.

Pauline's letters were more and more about God. In one dated May 15, 1965, she said, "Imagine how desolate our lives would be if God had not given the three of us each other."

As Jay Paul and I picked at our TV dinners, I felt we had already reached that desolation. Later she wrote: "Once, before Jay Paul was born, and you were so despondent, we went into a church and prayed for guidance. My dearest husband, I am convinced that some other power brought you and me together—and Jay Paul to be our son.

"Your creative talent is God-given, but you must make it work for you. You can control your talent now. It does not have to control you. God has given you just about everything—love, really true love from your wife—a son who worships you and above all, a brilliant, creative talent. Fight for what you have been given."

How could I fight when all the odds were against me?

On May 25, she wrote again: "My darling husband Jay, may God bless—guide—and be with you, as I am, every minute. Each day—and each considerate thing you do—makes my love profounder for you. What a marvelous man you are. We both need to renew our faith in God. We are really children in His hands, and we have learned what He gave us—and that we must cherish it. God bless you and our son."

Pauline's faith came through strongly in these letters. During our five years together I was aware of her love for God and her belief that He had brought us together for a purpose. But I was too self-centered to believe it myself. I felt we could and should make it on our own resources. No one should depend upon God to do things he could do for himself, I reasoned.

Meanwhile my life in a slum tenement as a bachelor father was proving to be very difficult. Everywhere I went Jay Paul went with me, clinging to my hand like a fragile limpet. But I was the least domesticated of men. The kitchen was a place of mystery and confusion to me.

The sisters at a nearby Roman Catholic church had been very helpful to us; we often left Jay Paul with them during emergencies. Now they suggested I should consider putting my son in a foster home.

When I mentioned this to Pauline on the telephone she was silent for a moment. "Maybe Mother can help us. Jay Paul would be much better off in the California sun than on the streets of New York. Besides, my mother would see that he got real nourishment to build him up." She said she would write her mother.

As soon as I could I traveled up to Saranac to visit Pauline, leaving Jay Paul to the ministrations of the sisters. My heart beat faster as I approached the graceful old Swiss chalet-style building. A nurse said Pauline could meet me in the sitting room. I walked into the brightly decorated room and at first couldn't find her. Then I reeled in shock. The patient I had thought was a little old lady was Pauline! My lovely wife was like a skeleton; her weight had dropped to ninety pounds. Her eyes were bright and glazed and sunk deeply into her head. I could see all of her delicate bone structure and it nearly broke my heart.

Hoping my shock didn't show, I quickly took her in my arms and kissed her. For a long moment we said nothing, it was just so good to be together again.

As usual, she tried to cheer me up. "The Lord is healing me,

Jay," she said. "The wonderful people here provide the medication, but God is doing it. You'll be surprised at how soon I'll be home."

I learned the prognosis for Pauline was twelve more months of treatment. Now I *had* to do something about Jay Paul. My mother-in-law solved the problem. Although 67, she climbed aboard a Greyhound bus in California and came nonstop across the country in four days. When I brought her to our apartment, I saw her wince. The place was a shambles—dirty dishes, filthy clothes, broken toys, toilet articles, and bric-a-brac scattered everywhere. Naomi drew a deep breath and went to work.

It was time for me to face hard facts. I was a total failure as far as Broadway was concerned. It wasn't going to happen. No one wanted me. The whole eastern trip had been a washout—a big mistake. All that mattered to me now was my wife and son.

Naomi, Jay Paul and I drove to Saranac Lake so Pauline could see her mother and son again before they returned to California. I would find a place to stay in Saranac near the hospital, possibly secure a part-time job somewhere nearby.

Since Pauline was very contagious, Jay Paul could not come inside the hospital. He stood on the lawn outside, looking up forlornly at his mother framed in a third-floor window. Naomi and I took turns visiting Pauline.

The good-bys were tearful and somber, but Pauline's determination and tenacity lifted me. "The Lord has my life in His hands," she said. "I don't mind it if He takes me, but I believe He is going to heal me." I just looked at her with tears in my eyes.

After putting Naomi and Jay Paul on a bus for Los Angeles, I drove back to our New York apartment and closed the place up for good. Everything that wouldn't fit into the old Buick was turned over to the Catholic nuns.

For a split second I puzzled over one item: the picture of Caligula. Pauline hated it and would have liked to get rid of it. Yet it represented my life's greatest triumph. I folded it up in an old blanket and placed it in the trunk of the car.

At Saranac I rented a room for $10 a week close to the hospital. After filing for unemployment insurance through my work qualification of the three-month bus and truck tour, I was awarded $50 a week. All of Pauline's hospital expenses were covered by my membership in the Screen Actor's Guild.

The crisis for Pauline came soon after my move to Saranac. One afternoon she had a sudden and severe reaction to the medication being pumped into her. Her body swelled up like a balloon; her skin turned fiery red. Since she was already just skin and bones, I expected she would die.

I walked around Saranac Lake during this emergency, my soul writhing in agony and bitterness. Once again fate was about to deliver me a cruel blow. The only prayer I could utter was negative; "Go ahead, God, stick it to me again. I know You're going to take Pauline away from me."

My soul was blackness; my thoughts were dark. All this was in contrast to the refreshing early summer scenes around me: the lake a sparkling blue, the sun rippling on its surface in incandescent, golden reflections, the joyous shouts of bathers splashing in the cool waters.

The next day Pauline was battling for her life, lying there pale and gasping for breath. Sitting helplessly by her side I saw her lips move. When I leaned forward I discovered she was not talking to me; she was praying. I felt left out, wondering if she was going to die right there before my eyes.

The following day was much the same. And the one after that. Pauline's tenacity of spirit was all that was keeping her alive. What a battler she was!

Her doctors were amazed and began to give me guardedly optimistic statements. "Your wife is remarkable . . . Great determination and recuperative powers . . . We can resume medication."

After another week the improvement was dramatic. The flush had left her cheeks, much of the feverish glitter was gone from her eyes. Even more importantly, there was the first definite weight gain.

The weeks went by and I gave up trying to find a part-time job. Instead I worked out a routine of two visits a day to the hospital, interspersed by long walks around the lake. My anger against life was gone; my violent resentment toward God had been replaced by an uneasy distrust. Pauline's faith had somehow been honored.

I decided that if there was a God, He was certainly capricious, favoring some and squashing others. It never occurred to me that I might find out more about Him by reading the Bible.

Summer ended and the foliage around Saranac Lake changed from a single and restful shade of green to a flaming mixture of reds, golds and browns. The leaves then dried up and dropped from the trees to provide a soft rustling carpet. The summer visitors had gone, leaving a much quieter village behind them.

More positive news came. Pauline's illness was arrested and her X-rays were proving negative. Her progress was so unusual that visiting doctors and medical students were brought to her bedside almost daily to observe a dramatic cure of modern medicine.

Pauline paid all due respect to the effects of the medicine and skill of the doctors. But she told me flatly that the cure had started when she had relinquished her life to the Lord. I nodded in agreement, feeling uneasy. Pauline assumed now that my faith in God was as strong as hers. I couldn't tell her that I was far from being a believer.

Snow began to fall and the winter crop of visitors arrived armed with skis, sleds and skates. Nights became long and exhilaratingly icy; daylight hours were short and subdued. But when the sun did penetrate beneath the layers of clouds and onto the fresh deposits of snow, Saranac took on the brightness of crystals scattered profusely across the ground and sprinkled like living beads of frosty light on every tree limb.

Pauline was now allowed out of the hospital for short periods and could visit me at the rooming house. She had gained forty pounds, reaching her desired weight of one hundred and thirty. Then she was given a release date—the day before Christmas. This was three months before the most optimistic estimate when she had entered the hospital the previous spring.

And so, on Christmas Eve, 1965, Pauline was released from Will Rogers Memorial, radiant, healthy, tears of joy in her eyes. We clung together fiercely. I had my Pauline back again.

We drove immediately to New York, checked into a small hotel for a few days while we made plans for the future. But the city still had one surprise punch to deliver.

In Manhattan, parking was then permitted on one side of a street, alternating daily. When we had arrived the evening before, I had found a lone space open. The next day I went outside to move the decrepit Buick to the other side of the street.

As I came up to our faithful old vehicle, I stopped in horror. It had been put up on wooden blocks; all four wheels were missing.

Cursing angrily, I opened the car door only to discover that both front and rear seats and the radio were missing. I pulled up the hood and once again recoiled in shock. The engine had been unbolted and stolen as well. In the trunk, it was the same—spare tire gone. Our car was stripped down to a shell.

Only one item had not been taken: the picture of me as Caligula.

Angrily, I removed it from the trunk. I then took off both license plates and threw them in the nearest trash can, a symbolic gesture against the city I now hated. New York had robbed us of our car; New York could dispose of the corpse.

A quick decision about the future was made: we turned our backs on the city that had given us such a fearful time, took our things to the bus station, and headed for Los Angeles and our little boy.

16

The Prodigal Returns

ON THE BUS RIDE to Los Angeles I had ample opportunity to review my life.

Assets: after thirty-five years, virtually nothing of material value. Now I even had to let my Screen Actor's Guild membership lapse, although without it we never could have paid for Pauline's treatment at Saranac Lake. I did have a recovered wife and a forlorn, homesick 5-year-old son. Furthermore, I had been off drugs now for more than five years.

Liabilities: a bad reputation in both Hollywood and New York which prevented me from getting work, a series of so many personal disasters that my confidence was near zero, and a lack of belief in anything other than that a person had to make it on his own.

There was another liability of which I was not aware. But I would feel its devastating impact before the year was half over.

At the Los Angeles bus station Jay Paul, Pauline's mother, her sister Margaret and her husband Elroy met us. An excited, joyful Jay Paul kept hugging and touching us. I was feeling part of a larger family again.

Since Naomi's house in Santa Ana was tiny, with only one small bedroom and an equally minuscule living room, Pauline and I again found ourselves sharing a single bed-sized couch each night. As I lay awake, balanced precariously over the iron rim of the sofa, I wondered if Pauline and I could ever look forward to sharing a double bed with a soft spring mattress.

Naomi was more than willing to share her possessions with us, what little she had, and I felt a growing love for this wonderful old lady who had absorbed the jolts and shocks of life with such grace and equanimity. But as the days passed, we knew we could not continue to impose on her hospitality much longer. We looked around for a place of our own.

Then an ad in the Santa Ana *Register* seemed to answer all our needs. The owner of a local building was advertising for a couple to manage and take care of an apartment house in return for free accommodations. We hastily applied.

The absentee owner, a Laguna Beach schoolteacher, prim, and with dark hair drawn back into a bun, looked us over carefully. Apparently satisfied, she hired us for the job. When we saw the building, we understood why she hadn't bothered to check us out more thoroughly.

At least fifty years old, the building was not only in disrepair, it was more of a rooming house than an apartment building. Situated in a seedy, rundown area of Santa Ana, the structure sat disconsolately on a lot overgrown with weeds.

It had twelve rooms, each rented on a weekly basis at $8 to $12 a room. Roomers came and left as rapidly as passengers in a downtown bus terminal. When we moved in and became accustomed to the building and its eccentricities, we discovered that all tenants had one thing in common: they were alcoholics. Our building was a flophouse for drunks and winos. In effect, we were their social workers.

Our small apartment was just inside a sagging porch. The screens all had holes, the floors were covered with old linoleum, hardly a square foot of paint remained free of chipping. This time our bed was a convertible sofa which had a broken spring that stuck me right in the middle of my back. That first night I groaned. *Was there not one single, solitary comfortable bed left in the world?*

Our job was to see that as many rooms as possible were occupied, collect the rents on time and see to the maintenance of the building and grounds. It sounded simple. But the building had developed a character of its own. Drunks arrived at all hours day and night whenever they wanted to sleep off a bender. If a door was open, they came inside to flop on a hallway or landing. The porch was also a good resting place; even the weeds would do in warm weather. The roomers were exclusively male. I had brought Pauline home to California to become the sole female in a flophouse for male drunks.

But if we were poor in Santa Ana, at least it was easier than being poor in New York. We could walk out our front door and look up at a friendly sun, taking good care of course not to fall through rotting porch planks.

Our tenants included some remarkable people. There were "Hughie" and "Dewie," two lovable drunks who roomed together, bound in inseparable companionship by their mutual love—love of the bottle, that is—and their occupation as hash-house fry cooks.

Both Hughie and Dewie were banjo players and would play loudly and sing with increasing resonance as they drank. The only time we ever saw them sober was when they went to work. Then they looked clean in their kitchen whites.

"The Engineer," age 70, was a loner. He liked to do his drinking by himself. When sober he would spin tales of driving steam-propelled monsters across desert and prairie and over mountains. When drunk, this old man was sweet, kind and an enemy to no one but himself. He would stagger down to our door, knock hesitantly and beg Pauline for a glass of milk and some crackers. Finally he would become so dehydrated, he would come down with the shakes and hallucinate, seeing all kinds of demons and monsters.

"The Screamer" was a quiet, subdued man who seemed to slink rather than walk. Most of the time he was so silent we didn't know when he was around. With a bottle, however, his screams would arouse the entire household and much of the neighborhood.

"Lou" was six-feet-six, handsome in a saturnine sort of way, and a gourmet cook. He made incredible meals of elegance and flavor and often took over Pauline's kitchen to do so. Then our pots and pans would boil and bubble with delicious aromas which brought all the tenants, mouths watering, as they followed their olfactory senses to our apartment. His dinners would often turn into an all-night bash.

Lou had a wealthy lady friend, a glamorous redhead, always immaculately coiffured. It was a peculiar relationship as most of the affection seemed to be on her part. At least when Lou was drunk it was that way, and he wasn't sober very often.

One day the sounds of quarreling came from his room; there was loud screaming from the lady followed by mad bull roars of rage from Lou. His front door had heavy, bevelled glass set into it. Suddenly the glass was shattered and Lou's lady friend shot out of the room with the drunken tenant in pursuit. His fingers caught her glamorous red curls and he pulled.

Lou stopped in shock, the lady kept going, minus her hair which was now firmly clasped in her boyfriend's right hand. We never did see the bald-headed lady again.

"Moonie" was a nickname we bestowed on a tenant we had never seen before. He came to the door dressed in a handsome suit and carrying a briefcase. His voice, well modulated, was that of an educated man. He paid two weeks rent in advance.

Then he retired to his room and started drinking. At first all was quiet and genteel. We did not see or hear from him again until several days later when the night was split asunder by hours of shouting, yelling and screaming. The well-turned-out businessman had deteriorated into a slobbering lunatic. We were forced to call the police. And it was now we discovered the anomalistic nature of the law.

When I had been arrested, police had come surging into my house in the best area of Los Angeles with drawn guns and dragged me off to jail in handcuffs. At the time I had been sitting quietly listening to records.

Here was a maniac keeping the whole neighborhood awake with his noise and swearing. But the police were powerless. They could do nothing, as he had paid the rent on his room. "Try and lure him out into the front yard," they said. "He comes under our jurisdiction there." But he would not budge from his room.

Needing additional income, I began looking for a part-time job. As I passed the "302 Cafe" in Santa Ana one morning, I happened to see a sign in the window—"COOK WANTED." Why not? I had tried almost everything else.

The head cook named Reno looked at me doubtfully, then hired me as a fry cook at $1.25 an hour, working the 11 P.M. to 7 A.M. shift. Only desperation got me into this ludicrous situation. I couldn't even fix a meal for myself at home.

Those who eat in cafes usually only see orders placed and food arriving at the table. Many people get quite upset if their order is not correct. But I learned what happens in between: the frantic attempt to keep each order straight; the heat and danger from boiling fat and water; the coarsely yelled orders from tired waitresses; the atmosphere of tension and pressure during which heads must remain cool if chaos is not to result.

I struggled and strained to learn the routines. My specialty was eggs over broken. No matter how I tried, this was the sad result.

The complaints yelled at our waitresses because of my incompetence were legion. But the girls stood up for me, made allowances for my lack of skill and, whenever possible, covered for me too.

One night the dishwasher broke down, ran over and flooded the floor of the kitchen, lapping around the stoves like a tidal wave. The floor boards on which I was standing were soon afloat and swirled around with every movement while I tried to cook eggs, bacon, sausages, ham and hash brown potatoes at the same time. I was slipping and sliding all over the place on the waterlogged boards, throwing things onto plates, juggling pans. It was sheer bedlam. All the time my white chef's cap was slipping over my eyes, blinding me.

As my skills improved, my pay increased to $1.55 an hour. I felt quite proud of myself. And then fate turned on me again.

I was walking home from work late at night when a car pulled up behind me. Three young hoodlums piled out and beat me up. My nose was badly broken. My wallet was taken. The beating continued for no reason other than sheer sadism. Fists pounded on my face, shoes kicked at my ribs and stomach.

I pretended a heart attack, clutching my chest.

One of the thugs said, "We don't want to kill him. Let's get out of here."

I staggered back to the rooming house, covered with blood. Pauline met me, aghast: "Jay, what happened?"

"I've been robbed," I gasped, "call the police!"

When they arrived, they took the necessary notes, asked the necessary questions. I heard nothing more from them.

My injuries kept me in bed for a couple of weeks and my job at the "302 Cafe" was taken by someone else. I wasn't too upset. It was pretty poor casting anyway—Caligula as a cook.

When I was well again, I went to the California State Employment Office to seek work. The counselor looked doubtful. "I'm afraid we have nothing here for actors. What else can you do?"

What could I do really except speak lines on screen or stage? I hesitated. "Well," I said, "I've been a fry cook and I'm great at cleaning monkey cages."

When he heard the latter, the clerk perked up. "As a matter of fact, there's an opening at the Fairview State Hospital in Costa Mesa. Some of the patients there need a great deal of care; they can't look after themselves." What he was saying in effect was, "Your experience in zoos might be useful."

He was quite right. Despite its modern and well landscaped exterior, Fairview was very much like a zoo inside; only the inmates were human instead of animal. Deformed and mentally inadequate souls, too freakishly terrible for the world to see, are tucked away out of sight.

My title was psychiatric technician trainee. As this was a civil service job, I had taken oral and written tests, passed a physical examination, been fingerprinted and appeared before a panel of examiners. My salary was $380 a month. As I put my fingers, one by one, on the block to be printed, my mind flashed back momentarily to the first time I'd undergone a similar experience: November 13, 1958, after my arrest in Bel Air.

Before being hired, I had thought I was to look after mentally retarded persons. But the reality was that I found myself in a live chamber of horrors. These poor, malformed creatures gibbered, screamed, and uttered animal howls continually. Some were such monstrosities I could hardly bear to look at them.

The risk of infectious hepatitis was so high, even our shoes had to be left in the changing room. At the end of the first day of work, I went home in total shock.

Some patients were microcephalic—tiny pinheads on grotesquely deformed and half-grown bodies, with twisted and equally deformed limbs. There were the hyperactives, running up and down all day long within their crib rails, howling like animals. It was my job to change their soiled bed linens and diapers. We bathed them in troughlike baths. They would not lie still but thrashed the water with their arms and legs until we were soaked clear through. The nightmare did not leave me during sleep that night. I suffered terribly.

Finally I was shown "The Head." He was called this because of his monstrous balloon-sized head with one eye set up in the forehead, the other down on the opposite cheek. His nose was pushed off center, overhanging an incredibly tiny mouth twisted in the direction opposite the nose. His arms and legs were long and simian. The huge head itself was supported in a sling, for its weight was too heavy for the body to bear. This poor soul was a man of 32.

"It's your turn to bathe 'The Head,' " I was told. I found it physically impossible to do.

One day, two men came to our apartment building asking for me. When Pauline said I was not in, one man left his card, asking that I get in touch with him as soon as I returned.

The card read: Santa Ana Police Department.

"What can all this be about?" I asked when I returned. We did not have a car, so it could not be a traffic ticket. Probably it had something to do with the gang of youths who had attacked me.

Pauline and I walked over to the Santa Ana Police Station with Jay Paul. We all needed some fresh air and the walk would do us good.

We were directed up to the second floor where I introduced myself. At the sound of my name one officer's head snapped up. He turned to me and said, "I must inform you that you are under arrest."

"Why?" I asked in stunned surprise.

He glanced down at a paper on his desk, then up to me. "There's

a bench warrant out on you," he said. "Seems you didn't appear
at a hearing in 1960 to set a new trial date."

"A new trial date?" I gasped. "I didn't even know about such
a thing."

"Well," he grunted, staring at the paper, "seems it was set after
they reversed your original conviction."

"But . . . but I never knew . . ." I started to protest; two men
stepped up, took my arms and hustled me toward a door.

Pauline began weeping and Jay Paul, hearing his mother cry,
joined in.

"I can't leave my wife and son," I pleaded. "They have no money;
who'll look after them?"

The detectives moved me along briskly. "Just come quietly with
us," one muttered.

They took me down into the old building's dank basement where
I was thrust into a holding tank. I collapsed in a corner and stared
at the grimy floor in bewilderment. No one had ever advised me
either by mail or in person that I was to appear at a hearing to
set a date for a new trial. A warrant had been out on me for six
years and this was the first time I ever heard a word about it.

Why had they waited until now? I wondered. I had been living
openly and was in the Los Angeles area at the time of the hearing.
My name was even appearing in the newspapers through my theatre
appearances.

Being unaware of the police purpose in getting me to the station,
I had brought no money, was dressed only in my work clothes,
and remembered too late that I had not endorsed my paycheck
from Fairview. As Pauline had no money, this presented a problem
for her. Since it was a Friday afternoon, no action would take
place in the courts during the weekend.

For three days I was crowded in a cell with thirty to forty other
men. There was only one toilet for all of us, right in the center of
the cell with no screens around it. There was no toilet paper and
the stench was abominable.

From time to time some tasteless food was pushed into the cell.
We ate like animals and as there was no way for daylight to enter,
the arrival of meals was the only way we could tell day from night.

I was held without bail, allowed no telephone calls or visitors, so I could not contact Pauline at all during that long and terrible weekend.

Early Monday morning when Pauline and Jay Paul came to the police station to see me, they ran into a stone wall of bureaucratic indifference. She told me later that the clerks and officials treated her as if she too were guilty of some crime, passing her from one to another, giving her no information or sympathy.

All weekend I had slept in my clothes without the benefit of a shower or a shave. Pale from the long weekend without daylight and smelling like an animal, I was manacled at both wrists and ankles and then chained in a long line to all the other lost souls. When I stumbled out from the dark basement into the glaring daylight with the other prisoners, I saw my wife and son gazing at me in sheer horror.

I jerked my head sideways, away from the boy, so he would not recognize his father and stumbled on with the others toward the waiting bus that would transport us to the Los Angeles County Jail. Pauline saw my effort to hide my face from Jay Paul and quickly covered his eyes with her hand.

After we had climbed aboard the bus and sank by pairs into the empty seats, I craned my neck to catch a last glimpse of Pauline. She stood transfixed in an evident state of shock. One hand was clamped tightly over Jay Paul's eyes, the other over her own mouth as if to suppress a scream of outrage.

17

Three Minutes
to Say Good-by

MY ARREST WAS exactly seven years to the day from the time I
had stood in Santa Monica Superior Court and heard myself declared guilty of drug possession. This verdict had later been overturned because of judicial error. What had gone wrong? I was a
prisoner again, held in chains like some dangerous animal.

Why was this happening to me? The minute I had been removed
from my family, the darkness had come back to my soul. Anger,
bitterness, hatred surged through me.

Was there one system of justice for the wealthy and influential,
another for the poor? When I owned a house in Bel Air, I was
released on bail in hours. Now that I had nothing, I had been
held incommunicado for three days and was being treated like the
worst of criminals. It was as if I lived in a totalitarian state.

Our destination was the Los Angeles County Jail, and I had
vivid memories of the sheer horror of that place. But there was a
surprise for me. The old jail was no longer in use; in its place
was a modern, sanitary facility. In fact, the new county jail was
almost antiseptic, with everything painted the same light shade of
green that psychiatric research probably advised was the color most
likely to soothe the criminal temperament.

From the holding tank it was the same old procedure, but now
it was accomplished in four hours instead of twenty-four. I was

assigned to my own cell right away, instead of to a mattress on the floor. I also had the luxury of a delousing shower and an issue of jail clothes.

On the following morning, I was awakened at 4:30 A.M. by a guard shouting, "Okay, Robinson, you're going to court." I was clean, but not shaven as I was taken back down to the basement, searched, chained to a line of prisoners and led to the bus.

My destination was the same Santa Monica Superior Court that had given me such nightmares before. It was as if the seven years had never happened. I was back in the same foul-smelling holding tank with the same obscenities inscribed on the walls.

When taken into court, I was seated. The district attorney stood up and gave the report:

"The defendant, Jay Robinson, appeared in this court in 1959 and was convicted of two counts of possession of narcotics. After reversal of the original conviction by the Second District Court of Appeals in April 1960, a hearing was held to set a date for a new trial. When the defendant did not appear at that hearing, a bench warrant was issued for his arrest. He was arrested in Santa Ana, California on May 13, 1966."

I stood there devastated.

"Do you have counsel or the means to pay for one?" the judge asked.

"I do not."

A public defender was then assigned to my case, a man I had never seen before and who knew nothing about me or the case. He wore a look of puzzlement, saying he would have to get the file.

The prosecutor then stood up. "I ask that he be held without bail."

Before I could react, I was on my way back to the basement holding tank. Later I was transferred back to the Los Angeles jail.

When the public defender came to see me at the jail the next morning, he pointed out that I should have gone back to the court to ask about my case, or at least contacted my lawyer. Pauline, I now remembered, had asked me to do this very thing. I had no explanation for my lawyer other than the whole thing had been such a soul-scarring experience that when I read that my conviction was reversed, I thought the whole terrible mess was over and done with.

"How did all this come up again after so long?" I asked him.

"The fingerprints taken for your job at Fairview State Hospital bounced out of the computer in Sacramento."

"But don't you see?" I protested. "If I had known about the bench warrant, I would never have let them fingerprint me."

He agreed. "There was obviously no intent on your part to avoid trial."

When she came to visit me, Pauline said that she had spent two days trying to find me. Without a car she had gotten up early in the morning and bussed all over the Los Angeles area from one office to another, lugging a big suitcase of more than a thousand newspaper clippings and documents she had found in our belongings. These proved that I had been in full public view during the past six years. There were even advertisements about me in the Santa Monica *Outlook,* published in the same city as the court which had issued the bench warrant. She told officials that I had no knowledge of the warrant for my arrest and the court could have found me easily if they had looked. Nobody was interested.

In court two days later the public defender asked for my release on my own recognizance. The district attorney insisted that I be kept in custody. After hearing arguments from both sides, the judge set bail at $1,500. For us this was impossible. However, Pauline's sister, Margaret, and her husband, Elroy, were able to put up their house as security. It was all they owned. On Memorial Day, May 30, 1966, after a total of seventeen days and nights of torment in jail, I was released on bail and rejoined my family.

The joy of freedom was tempered by the sobering fact that I still had to face trial on the same old charge of possessing drugs seven years before. "Throw yourself on the mercy of the court," the public defender advised. "With all your years of clean living taken into account, if you plead guilty, you'll probably get off with probation."

It was sound advice and Pauline urged me to follow it. "Jay," she pleaded, "I really feel this man knows what he's talking about.

Please take his advice." But I didn't agree. My mind worked furiously. I was no criminal. I had seen that drugs were a trip to nowhere and had gotten off. It wasn't fair that I be tried again now after all these years.

I had heard of a brilliant lawyer named Huntley Briggs who had a reputation for winning cases for defendants regardless of how guilty they seemed. I didn't want to confess and throw myself on the court's mercy. The courts I had been in had certainly shown no mercy to me. I wanted my freedom now.

As Huntley Briggs listened to my story, and looked through my enormous box of press clippings, his eyes glistened. The glow faded somewhat when he discovered I had no money to pay a lawyer. He thought for a moment, then stood up and walked about our small, dismal-looking apartment. With his flashy sports car, his expensive clothes and flamboyant manner, he seemed totally out of place in our drab surroundings.

With a casual wave of his hand, he came to a decision, "I'll take your case for nothing. The publicity I receive for getting your case dismissed will be my payment."

I was jubilant and felt like hugging him.

"When I present this mountain of material in court, it will show conclusively that no attempt was made to locate you. The judge will have to dismiss the case," he assured me.

I thanked the public defender for his help and retained Huntley Briggs as my lawyer. After several more court appearances my trial was set for October.

During the summer, we were a family again, living now in a small apartment in Santa Ana. Pauline got a job as a dental assistant, while I began working for a veterinarian. I was back cleaning animal cages once more.

Jay Paul was now 5 and getting ready to start kindergarten in the fall. Pauline had been a good mother; despite all the adversity, our son was obedient and well-mannered. As he ran and played with other children in our neighborhood, I felt a surge of pride. We would get through the trial; I would be cleared, then I would get on with my acting career. As I looked at the picture of Caligula which I had put up on the wall of our breakfast room, I thought: "When all this is over, I'll be a star again."

But I was worried about Pauline. She had lost some weight; there were more lines in that finely chiseled face; those expressive eyes were often rimmed with fatigue. One night I tried to cheer her up.

"When this is all over, I'm going back to films. That's where I belong." We were sitting in the breakfast room and I stared at Caligula on the wall.

Pauline shook her head. "I wish I could believe that you'll be going back to anything, Jay. Somehow I don't feel right about your new lawyer."

"He's going to get me out of this, that's all. The public defender would have me back in jail again."

"But Jay, you're not trusting the Lord. In my heart I feel this new lawyer is taking the wrong approach. He'll have you saying things that aren't true."

I just shook my head. "People like us get clobbered unless we use our wits. Look what's happened to me because we're broke. The court treats me like scum."

Pauline's eyes suddenly filled with tears. "Please don't talk that way, Jay. I know you've been hurt, but we have to have faith."

"You have faith, Pauline. It works for you. It doesn't for me."

"Jay, when we were at Saranac Lake, you seemed to believe. You prayed. You agreed that God healed me. Why have you changed?"

"I'm not saying that there isn't a God," I said defensively. "I've wanted to believe all my life, but none of my prayers has ever been answered."

"That isn't true. You prayed for me. My health was restored."

I was getting uncomfortable. "God answered your prayers, Pauline. I tried to pray, but it was hypocrisy. You can't pray if you don't believe."

Pauline's sobs stabbed me. I got up and awkwardly put my arm around her. "I'm sorry if I hurt you, Dear. But I can't go on pretending I'm a Christian when I'm not."

"Then how can you pretend you were innocent of the charge of drug possession when you were not?"

That one hurt. I said nothing. Pauline stared at me stonily for awhile, then her face softened.

"I don't understand you, Jay; you're a kind, faithful husband. I know you love me and Jay Paul, that you would even die for us. But every now and then, some dark force takes over your life. Then you're so self-centered and selfish that I don't know you." She glanced up to the picture on the wall. "I think it goes back to that Caligula part."

"That's nonsense, Pauline. You have a thing about that role. I haven't been Caligula for years."

"I'm not so sure. You're very changeable."

"Pauline, let me try to explain: I'm not an atheist; I believe there's a God; but He's not . . . not real to me. I don't think He likes me. If He did, He wouldn't have let me go through such misery and grief. I wish I could believe that God loves us, but I've seen too many miserable, wretched, hurting people to believe that He does."

Pauline stared at me helplessly. "He loves us if we let Him."

I just shook my head.

Fall arrived, the date for the trial was at hand. I became suddenly aware of the fact that the prosecutors were young and bright with all the resources of the state of California behind them, while my defense was to be conducted by a flamboyant but erratic man whom I had seen very little in the past four months. He was utterly confident; I was suddenly very nervous.

For one thing, there was the incident that had happened in the judge's chambers shortly before we went to trial. I had gone with Briggs and the district attorney for arguments on a motion Briggs had filed for dismissal. The motion had been based on the premise that there was gross negligence on the part of the warrant division in not bringing me in even though I had been in full public view for six years following the order for my rearrest.

We arrived at the judge's offices only to have Briggs botch his presentation badly. He had all the material in his briefcase which Pauline had so carefully collected, but when he presented his case to the judge, the material was submitted in a disorganized and confusing way.

The judge looked at the multitude of clippings, press releases and advertisements, none of which were in order and many of which were undated. The presecutor objected to the motion and presented his arguments.

"Motion denied," the judge intoned after both sides had been heard.

Instead of having the case dismissed, I found myself facing a retrial on the original charge against me.

And then it was time.

As I arrived outside the courtroom, I had my first shock. A man passed me saying, "Hello, Jay. How are you?"

It was the informer who had testified against me during the first trial. I learned later that the authorities had tracked him down in northern California to serve as a prosecution witness.

When the proceedings began, Briggs had not appeared. The judge was obviously annoyed. "Where is your lawyer, Mr. Robinson?" he asked.

All I could do was shake my head.

Huntley Briggs arrived fifteen minutes later as the judge fumed. But not the prosecutors. I saw them smiling confidently to each other.

As Briggs fumbled through his papers, the trial got underway. The chief prosecutor, who appeared to be very sure of himself, called the same witnesses as before. The narcotics officers who arrested me repeated their stories. The narcotics evidence was presented again. The informer gave his same deadly testimony. The proceedings dragged on.

A week went by as the trial continued. In steady sequence it seemed to unfold just as my previous trial had, seven years before.

Huntley Briggs consistently was late. Always he seemed to be unprepared. When it finally came time for me to testify, I stonily repeated the lie that I had been framed and that the drugs were planted in my bathroom.

I was very disappointed in my lawyer's summary. Several times he had to stop and fumble through his papers. His presentation lacked clarity and coherence. I felt that he left out some important facts. But when he finished, he winked at me and seemed very confident.

The jury was out for only a few hours. Then we were all called back to the courtroom to hear the verdict.

I stood up feeling confident now that the verdict this time would be in my favor. I glanced at Huntley. He smiled at me. "You'll be acquitted," he whispered.

"What is your verdict?" the judge asked the foreman of the jury. "Guilty."

The word shattered me like a grenade explosion.

I turned to see Pauline lower her head.

The judge then continued my bail until sentencing. I was told that a probation officer would interview me and make his recommendation to the court regarding sentence.

Throughout both trials, I had persistently professed my innocence, denying all the charges. The probation officer was most sympathetic and disarming, throwing a loaded question at me in the friendliest manner possible. "Now that it's all over, tell me the truth. Were those your drugs in the bathroom?"

Was it naivete, confusion, or that perverse imp inside me that made me answer the truth? "Yes," I replied trustingly.

His report generously recommended that I be granted straight probation with no further time to serve. But his analysis of my situation contained my admission of guilt.

The judge read the probation report as I stood before him several days later. Suddenly he exploded. "By not admitting the truth, you have wasted the court's time and the state's money!" He threw the probation report onto his desk and glared at me. "Not only am I *not* granting you probation; I'm giving you the maximum sentence called for by law."

He paused. "On the first count: the time prescribed by law." BANG! went his gavel.

"On the second count: the time prescribed by law." BANG! It amazed me that the gavel's handle didn't break.

"Remanded to custody," were his final words.

I was stunned. "What does that mean—time prescribed by law?" I asked my lawyer.

"Two to ten years," was Huntley's terse reply. He rose, stuffed his papers into his briefcase, snapped the lid closed and left. I could hear Pauline sobbing nearby.

The bailiff came up to us. "All right, Robinson." There was no "Mister" now. I was a convicted felon on my way to state prison.

"You have three minutes to say good-by," he said.

Above: Pauline, Jay's wife, in 1953 at age 22, about the time *The Robe* was being filmed. She and Jay met seven years later. *Right:* January 15, 1962— Jay and Pauline on the opening night of *Caligula* in Miami. Again the portrayal of the mad emperor was to bring disaster upon Jay.

Left: In 1962 Jay portrayed Hamlet during a Shakespeare festival in Miami. Much of his agony was yet to come. *Below:* Jay Paul in 1964. This picture was taken during Jay and Pauline's toughest years of married life in New York City. Jay was unable to find work and Pauline was ill with tuberculosis.

Jay, Pauline, and Jay Paul in 1970. Now 40 and out of prison, Jay was trying valiantly to climb back up the ladder of acting success. Although persistent and determined, he was only partially successful. His meeting with Christ was still eight years away.

Left: With William Shatner, left, in an episode of "Star Trek," 1968. *Below:* Jay in makeup for a role in *Planet of the Apes,* 1973.

Top left: Jay as "Dracula" in *Train Ride to Hollywood,* 1974. *Top right:* Jay, as "Shylock" from Shakespeare's *The Merchant of Venice,* a television role he played in 1975. *Below:* Jay plays Dr. Shrinker, a mad scientist with his "incredible shrinking machine" in an ABC network hit television series for children, 1976.

Father and son in 1975 when Jay Paul was 14 years of age.

Jay, as President Lincoln, delivering the Gettysburg Address in 1976 in a stage appearance at the Los Angeles Sports Arena during a presentation honoring the Bicentennial.

Below: Jay Robinson, George Brent, and Dean Jones on the set of *Born Again* in early 1978. *Right:* Jay with Chaplain Jamieson Matthias at Chino prison during the filming of *Born Again.* Chaplain Matthias had befriended Jay and been a source of strength during his imprisonment at Chino.

Above: Jay and Pauline with Paul Temple, associate producer of the movie *Born Again,* and his wife, Karen (right), in 1978. *Below:* In a scene from *Born Again,* Dean Jones as Charles Colson and Jay Robinson as Colson's attorney, David Shapiro, stand for Colson's sentencing.

Jay Robinson, right, as David Shapiro and Dean Jones as Charles Colson in a scene from *Born Again*. This scene, filmed in Washington, D.C., shows the U.S. Capitol in the background.

Above: A reborn Jay Robinson with his new brother in Christ, Charles Colson, during filming of *Born Again*—the story of Colson's life during the Washington political scandal known as Watergate. (Photo by John Monte.) *Below:* Ruth Carter Stapleton (center) with Jay and Pauline in early 1979.

Jay with Bette Davis—"Congratulations, Jay, for an inspirational book, for one and all who fall by the wayside."

18

"The Big House"

THE THICK, STEEL BARS of a large gate loomed up ahead through the windshield of the jail bus in which I was once again chained like an animal. There was a hush in the bus now. The idle chatter had fallen away to a somber silence. This was the Reception Guidance Center at Chino, California, the clearing house for the state's entire penal system, where inmates are introduced to prison discipline before being assigned to more permanent locations.

Slowly and smoothly, the gate opened through some remote electrical control, and the bus edged through into a courtyard where men with guns cradled in their arms took up positions around us. As we filed out of the bus, shuffling in our leg irons, I could see we were inside two tall barbed wire fences that apparently circled the prison. At intervals along the fence stood high guard towers. From the one closest to us we could see a rifle barrel aimed at us.

Before us a heavy steel door set in a massive concrete wall slid sideways and our long line of chained men shuffled inside. The whirring, grinding noise that followed was from the door closing behind. Then came a clanging dull thud as it slammed shut. It was one of the most depressing and menacing sounds I had ever heard in my life. I realized at last why prisons are often referred to as the "slammer." Chino had just slammed shut on my life.

First our chains were removed, then we were ordered to take off all our clothes. Soon I stood in my skinny nakedness with forty others. You take nothing into prison with you.

"You are now in state prison," the guard barked. "In case any of you start thinking of escape, I want you to know you are surrounded by gun towers in which are trained guards with thirty-o-six rifles. They are excellent shots. You'd never make it over the first barbed wire fence.

"You are about to be given a number. As far as we're concerned, that's your name from now on." The finality of what he was saying clawed at my heart. "If you have any money with you, your clothes can be mailed home. If not, dump everything in this barrel. It'll be sent to the Salvation Army."

My clothes went into the barrel and I felt a twinge of anguish, for I stood now like some prehistoric man, all traces of my personality stripped from me.

I moved to a counter where a sergeant issued me my new name— number B5985 which was instantly recorded in the California State Prison records, by computer extension to FBI Headquarters in Washington and to any police department in the country that requested it. With this number I lost my right to vote for the rest of my life. I had in effect been stripped of my citizenship.

Still naked, I was herded along the counter, behind which convict clerk-typists in California prison blues were processing inmates' personal records. Against the wall was a line of wooden benches on which sat a stone-faced group of convicts looking over the new crop of naked prisoners. I did not know it at the time, but this was a "selection panel," scouting out vulnerable, fragile types for possible future homosexual relations. Signs of effeminacy were being mentally noted and stored away for the prison grapevine.

The Reception Guidance Center at Chino is built around what must be one of the longest corridors in the world; the cell blocks open on either side—like a huge comb with teeth on both sides of its spine. The corridor is broken into controllable sections every hundred feet or so by sliding, steel-barred doors. When I first walked down this interminable corridor, the steel barriers slid open before me but only after the ones behind me had thudded shut. These cell blocks had names like dormitories at a boys' school. I was assigned to one called "Cypress."

Each cell at Chino is equipped for two men. At that time whites were paired with whites, blacks with blacks, and Chicanos with Chicanos. My roommate was a surly, taciturn, older man named Jack, whose communication was constantly studded with obscenities. From the beginning we went about our routines ignoring each other. I soon discovered that noise and bedlam prevailed inside prison. Loudspeakers constantly barked orders and prisoners' numbers. Steel doors were constantly slamming shut; the lights were on constantly. Almost every hour we were forced to stand by our cell doors for a head count.

A bell clanging loudly summoned us to the mess hall. The food, served by fellow prisoners, was somewhat better than the slop we had at the county jail.

Each prisoner was assigned to a counselor whose job it was during a six-week evaluation period to recommend what be done with him while in prison. Maximum security prisons such as San Quentin and Folsom are dreaded. Minimum security places such as forestry camps are most sought after despite the hard, back-breaking work.

And then a marvelous thing happened to me! A kind lady by the name of Mrs. Lucie Bird was appointed my counselor. With her gentle black face and compassionate eyes, I felt I was in the presence of an angel.

After my first interview she said with deep concern, "You don't belong here, Mr. Robinson." She did everything she could to get me released. Her report on me was laudatory and she even wrote to the sentencing judge, asking him to reconsider, which he refused to do.

One day she came to me, her face alight with smiles. "I have such good news for you, Mr. Robinson."

I could hardly stand the suspense. "Are they going to let me out, Mrs. Bird?" I asked.

"No. But something almost as good. You were sentenced to two to ten years, but you come under the old laws of seven years ago so your actual sentence is only six months to ten years. You could be eligible for parole at the end of six months and I'm certainly going to recommend that."

The date came for Pauline's first visit, and I was keyed up almost beyond endurance with excitement. When my number was called, I was shown to a small cubicle; Pauline was seated in a similar cubicle facing me. But we were separated by a thick sheet of shatter-proof glass and could not touch or communicate. A phone was hanging on a hook on my cubicle wall. Picking it up I was able to talk to her via a phone on her side of the glass. All calls were monitored by guards at phones in a control booth. It was an awkward way to talk and I could see that Pauline was uncomfortable. There were dark shadows under her eyes, her hair was wind-blown and her mouth was tense.

"Tell me about Jay Paul," I began.

"He's fine, Jay. He likes school and has made some new friends. He's interested in baseball."

"Are you two comfortable at your mother's?"

"It's working out okay. Naomi is so thoughtful. She reads to Jay Paul a lot."

We went on talking about our everyday lives. I explained the prison routine, described Mrs. Bird and reported the good news that I would be eligible for parole in six months.

Pauline brightened. "Oh, Jay. That would be so good. Two years seems a lifetime but ten years is an eternity."

Tears suddenly filled her eyes, her lips began trembling and she struggled to get her smile back in place. I suddenly knew she was holding back something.

"Pauline, what's troubling you?"

My wife was struggling for composure. She drew a deep breath, clenched the phone tighter and blinked back the tears. "I do have some bad news. They've found cancer in my uterus and want to operate right away."

For a few moments I just stared at her. It couldn't be true. My lovely, faithful, devoted wife—how could this terrible thing happen to her? "Are you sure?" I asked weakly.

"Yes, Jay. There have been X-rays, tests, the works."

"Then you knew about this during my trial."

"Yes."

"Why didn't you tell me?"

Pauline stared back, tears glistening in her eyes. "I couldn't give you anything more to worry about then, Jay."

I looked at my wife numbly. All the time she had been walking over the vast distances in Los Angeles, hauling a heavy bag of clippings and documents to plead my case, she had been fighting her own battle too. As I thought of this sick, frail woman being scorned and rebuffed by an unfeeling, uncaring bureaucracy, my head began to pound and bile rose so thick in my throat I could hardly talk.

"When will they operate?"

"I don't know."

"What can we do, Pauline? How will you get proper medical care? We have no money at all."

"Don't worry, Jay. My family will help out. God will be with me."

The bell rang for the end of visiting time and as my wife got up to go, my last vision of her burned itself into my memory. For Pauline was white-faced, tired and ill. Bravely she tried to smile. Once again, I felt I was about to lose her. The cruelty of the world overwhelmed me. Why did someone as pure and innocent as Pauline have to suffer so much?

19

At the Gladiator School

MRS. BIRD CAME TO see me one day with a worried look on her face. I braced myself for more bad news about Pauline.

"You are being transferred, Jay."

"Where to?"

"Up north to Tracy. It's called the Deuell Correctional Center."

"How far north is Tracy?"

"About four hundred miles."

This was a new and terrible blow. At Chino, Pauline was only an hour's bus ride away. A separation of four hundred miles would completely eliminate the visits.

"Is there any news about Pauline?" I asked. The operation was to take place any day now.

"Nothing new, Jay."

Then my heart sank as I realized I was also losing Mrs. Bird as my counselor. This sensitive, compassionate woman had become a close friend. "It's killing me to lose you as a counselor and the visits of my wife too. Is there any way to get a postponement or a reversal of this decision?" I asked.

"I'll do the best I can, Jay. I've already asked for a stay of your transfer. But you know how it is. Once a decision is made, it's almost impossible to get it reversed." She went on to explain that they needed clerk-typists at Tracy, that my name had been on a list of availables and that Tracy had put in a request for me.

I groaned helplessly. When typing up my personnel record, the prison official had asked for my job classification. "Actor" wouldn't do, he said, and suggested "clerk-typist." When I stated that I could not type, he had shrugged. That lie would cost me visits with Pauline.

From the other prisoners I learned that Tracy was called the "Junior San Quentin," that it had a trade training center for the toughest young prisoners. And because there was so much weight lifting and physical conditioning, it was known as the "Gladiator School." That was the most ironic news of all. Caligula was going to the Gladiator School.

Several days later I was processed out of Chino, chained and herded into a prison bus called the "Grey Goose," for a thirteen-hour ride to Tracy, California.

By now I was 36 years old and instead of being at the height of my acting career, I was a four-digit number being shuffled about the California prison system. Every time I thought that nothing worse could happen to me, it did. My wife needed me as never before, but I couldn't sit by her bed and hold her hand as I had done at Saranac Lake. I couldn't even call her on the telephone. And now, I had lost the one link between us—Mrs. Bird. My soul was in torment; inside me darkness had completely taken over.

As I stared bitterly out the bus window, a Cadillac convertible passed. I saw it was the same model as the one I had owned, except mine had been plated in fourteen-carat gold. Grimly, I compared myself to the well-dressed young man driving. He was steering in a relaxed manner, one hand on the wheel. His free arm was draped around the shoulders of a girl sitting next to him. Her head was cradled lovingly on his shoulder and her long blonde tresses streamed out behind them in the wind.

Inside the Grey Goose, the seats were rock hard with short, straight backs. Both our hands and feet were manacled; prisoners were secured together by a long chain running the entire length of the bus. We were also handcuffed in pairs by the wrist. If someone had to relieve himself on the long trip, a guard would have to release not only the convict but also his seatmate and both, still handcuffed together, would then shuffle to the toilet at the rear of the bus.

The toilet was only partially concealed by an open wire mesh screen. Both men would have to be in the toilet at the same time, with the guard also keeping an eye on them to insure there was no attempt at escape. The stench rising from such primitive arrangements was heavy, overlaying the body odors emanating from some forty men, none of whom had been allowed a shower that morning.

We were under constant observation all through the trip from heavily-armed guards at the front and rear of the bus. Because of all this security, I was startled to discover that my seatmate was slyly picking at his handcuffs with what looked like a hairpin. How he had managed to smuggle it aboard the Grey Goose was beyond me. Before leaving Chino we had been stripped and searched in the usual embarrassing prison manner, and then provided with clothes which were to be worn only on the buses—a pair of white cotton trousers secured by a drawstring and a baggy white shirt. My shoes had large "Vs" notched at the heel, and my number was stenciled on the instep for identification.

Meanwhile my seatmate was calmly picking away at the locks of his manacles with a hairpin, the activity of course concealed from the guards. If he were to free himself and bolt for freedom, I would be considered an accomplice.

I sat there paralyzed with fear, glancing out of the corners of my eyes at his progress.

"What are you doing?" I hissed.

He spoke calmly, not looking at me and keeping his lips almost motionless, like a ventriloquist. "Just take it easy, man," he said. "I've done this before. I'm going to open these cuffs."

"But that's stupid," I whispered. "You can't go anywhere. And I want no part of it."

"Relax. You haven't seen anything. Act as if you knew nothing about it."

"But what will you do if you get them open?"

He was nonchalant in his reply. "When the bus stops, I'll get off."

"With irons on your legs?"

"I'll worry about that later. Now shut your mouth."

His whisper carried such malevolence that I did the only thing left open to me; I feigned sleep. But I did peer from under nearly closed eyelids.

With a start I saw that he had freed the handcuff securing him to me. This released him from the chain binding us to the other prisoners. Now he was working on the cuff attached to his other wrist.

Suddenly, I heard him hiss with alarm. The guard was coming down the aisle of the bus. He pushed the unlocked cuff against mine, then looked out of the window at the passing scene, the hairpin palmed out of sight.

The guard gave us a cursory inspection and passed on. My seat-mate then resumed his efforts to open the other lock.

But as the hours passed, it would not give. He sat in a frenzy of perspiration, beads of sweat oozing down his forehead until his face seemed coated in an oily film.

"Oh, no!" he groaned, "what am I going to do?" He had been trying in vain now to relock the one cuff he had successfully opened. We were fast approaching Tracy.

Then we came to a large sign reading, "A California State Prison. Deuell Correctional Center, Tracy, California." Behind it was a big, low-lying, dull grey factory-type building. We were there.

As we were processed by the guards, my former seatmate desperately held his unlocked handcuff together, hoping to avoid detection. But when it came our turn to have the manacles removed, the guard swore in anger.

"We've got a wise guy here," he said in a loud voice. Immediately all eyes turned on the guilty man as he stood there trembling.

"You haven't been here two minutes, and already you're in deep trouble." The luckless prisoner was hustled away and I never saw him again. To my surprise, no one ever questioned me about the incident.

In Tracy the cell blocks were called "units." I was assigned to "Unit E" where, as a member of the adult work crew, I was given a single cell. This was my first privacy in months. Generally, such solitude is not valued by prisoners since there is no one to talk to or play cards with when locked up.

Tracy was different than Chino in many ways. At Chino we had gone to showers in groups, usually stripping off our clothes in our cells and walking to the shower room draped in towels. Soon after my arrival, a guard pounded on my cell door with his heavy club. "Want a shower, Robinson?" he called.

"Yes, thank you," I yelled back and stripped off my clothes. When my door was released, I stepped out of my cell, tying my towel around my waist. As I did so, the cell door was locked automatically behind me.

And then it happened. The sight of a skinny, pale guy wearing only a towel brought Unit E into an uproar. The place erupted with catcalls, wolf whistles and raucous cheers.

I stood paralyzed. There was no way to retreat to my cell, so I strode to the shower room and away from the embarrassing uproar. From then on I walked to my showers fully clothed and undressed inside.

The young prisoners at Tracy had a rolling, strutting type walk, rather like sailors ashore for the first time after months at sea. Most wore "boneroos"—slick, neatly pressed blues which were pulled up high on the chest, zoot-suit style. They were out to impress others with their hardness. Their message: "Hey, man! Don't mess with me, or you'll get hurt." They were always bragging about their expensive homes, cars, money and success with women on the outside. If half of what they claimed could be believed, we must have had hundreds of Rockefellers in Tracy.

"Fish" were newcomers, and this group of course included me. It is a descriptive term as I felt very much like a fish out of water.

"Punks" were young kids whose fragility and vulnerability made them easy prey for aggressive homosexual advances.

Older than most of these young gladiators, I played the part of a stooped, aging and sallow Gunga Din, exaggerating the role to make sure there was nothing attractive about me.

There were two main types of homosexual prisoners, and I soon learned to recognize them on sight. "Jocks" were hard, tough types, while "queens" were effeminate, plucked their eyebrows and made up their eyes with the charcoal from burnt matches. The jocks would play the tough role and the queens would sort of simper around with exaggerated feminine walks.

The guard on the daytime shift in Unit E was a tall, stringy man named Cooper. He rarely revealed the slightest trace of human feeling, keeping his face expressionless at all times. I wondered what sort of man he was outside of prison. Did he love a wife and family, or was he the same automaton off duty as he was around the cellblock? Cooper was the kind of man who would respond to a violent death in his vicinity with a blank, disinterested look and the flat, unemotional order: "Okay, get him out of here. We've got to keep the place clean."

A spit and polish man, Cooper wore white gloves to detect dust in the cells. Offenders got a "write-up" and loss of privileges. Write-ups took two forms. Any prisoner found guilty of not shaving, walking in the corridors with shirttails out or having any dirt or dust in the cell got a "128." This went only on the prisoner's record in the Tracy card files.

A "115" was much more serious. Given for more serious infractions such as bringing extra food from the mess to one's cell, fighting, or disobedient behavior, a "115" went into the inmate's permanent state prison file and could postpone parole for a year.

There was a subdued air of violence hanging over Tracy. Part of it was racial, part came naturally from the violent natures of the prisoners. One day in the mess hall a young prisoner seated next to me calmly reached out and took some food off the tray of an older man across from him. Just as calmly the older man lifted his fork and with all his strength stabbed the offender through the back of the hand. I could hear the bones and tendons of his hand crunch, as spurts of blood shot across the steel tabletop.

The injured man screamed, then sat paralyzed, his face ashen with shock. At the sound, all conversation in the dining hall stopped. When guards took the two antagonists away, talk resumed again as if nothing had happened. In fact, many men did not even stop eating to see what had caused the screams.

As soon as I arrived at Tracy I tried to contact Pauline. We were not allowed long distance telephone calls except in real emergencies, and then only collect calls could be made. I wrote daily letters, asking for news.

The days passed and my fears grew. I kept seeing Pauline's white face on the operating table and the grim-faced doctors shaking their heads. I had gone through this before at Saranac Lake and had expected the worst then. Despite her recovery, my negative outlook had not changed. I had no more hope than I did before. I tried to pray, but it was a mockery. To whom was I praying? To a God who created His people only to make them suffer?

I tried attending the chapel. One Sunday the chaplain delivered a sermon in near medical terms describing the suffering of Jesus on Calvary. He talked about the breaking of His bones as the flesh was pierced and the nails hammered home, of His tongue protruding and eyes bulging out, of fever and of agony. It was a very graphic description delivered in layman's terms, and made an indelible impression on me. This Jesus certainly knew what suffering was all about. But why did God put His own Son and most of His children through such pain? In one part of the Bible, God promised abundance and well-being; in another part He says that to follow Him we have to pick up the cross. It all seemed confusing and contradictory.

Of one thing I was certain; Pauline would be praying. I rested my hopes for her recovery on her prayers.

The letter arrived several days later. From the handwriting, I knew it was from my wife. I tore open the envelope, my hands shaking.

Dearest Jay:

God has been good to us again! The operation was a success. The doctor said that he is pretty sure that all the cancerous cells were removed. I am rejoicing and I know you are too.

Do you see, Jay, how God answers our prayers? He healed me at Saranac Lake. He did it again here in Los Angeles. We must be grateful.

The world has no meaning without God. He loves us so very much,

Jay. I want more than anything else in the world for you to feel His
love . . .

I read the letter with tears of joy. My patient, loving, courageous
wife had battled back again. First tuberculosis. Now cancer. What
a fighter! How much I loved her!

20

Easter Sunday

EASTER CAME EARLY in 1967—on the 27th of March. It began no differently than any other Sunday. The awakening bell sounded at 7 A.M. I washed, shaved and was ready for the breakfast bell an hour later. The food was a little better than usual—eggs.

Next to me was a young Chicano prisoner in boneroos. He stared at me several times, then asked, "Is your name Robinson?"

"That's right."

"The actor."

I nodded again.

"You must be the guy in that movie they're showing on TV tonight—*The Robe.*"

I had heard about it earlier in the week. A bulletin had circulated to all prison units announcing the showing. In the recreation room an inmate had tossed me the television page of a local newspaper with a large advertising feature on this special television film presentation. It left me with mixed feelings: resurging ego and pride over my former stardom and uneasiness at how this notoriety would affect my prison status.

Back in my cell, I pondered whether I should make a special request to see it. It was not my night to watch television; newcomers to prison are given limited TV privileges. My chain of thought was interrupted by a startling announcement over the prison PA system:

"Robinson—B5985: You have a visitor. Report to control."

I almost fell on the floor in surprise. Who could that be? Not Pauline. She would still be recuperating from her operation.

At control, they checked me out and passed me along to the visiting area. A guard there said, "Okay, Robinson. In there. You know what to do."

"No, I don't," I said frantically. "This is my first visitor."

"Strip for a skin search."

I hurriedly removed my clothing as every second now counted toward my visiting time. Once again every orifice and patch of hair on my body was searched, and only then was I admitted to the visiting area.

At the door I was told, "You are allowed one quick kiss when you meet, and then you must not touch again until leaving."

It must be Pauline. My heart leaped as I saw her advancing across the room toward me. Our first kiss in four months! She looked pale and wan, but that warm loving light was back in her luminous brown eyes.

Now I understood the body search. There was no plate glass to separate us from each other at Tracy. We were allowed to sit and talk across a table from each other in the prison visiting room. Other prisoners at tables scattered about the room were enjoying the same privilege.

"Jay," said Pauline. "A terrible thing happened to me on the way into the prison."

"What was that?"

"I had to pass through a metal detector and I forgot that I had a jar of coins in my purse. They set off alarm bells and I was taken out of line for a search."

Pauline's face was so serious that I had to laugh. Soon we were both doubled up with hilarity over gentle Pauline being put under surveillance.

"Why were you carrying a jar of coins?"

"They're my tips as a waitress."

"A waitress? When did you begin that?"

"A week ago. We needed the money, Jay. I told God in my prayer that I would take the first job that came along. The next day there was an ad in the help-wanted column for a waitress."

"But so soon after your operation."

Pauline smiled reassuringly. "It wasn't so bad. I'm okay, Dear."

I shook my head in dismay. "It hurts me to have you in a job where you're on your feet all the time."

I asked how she had made the four hundred-mile trip north.

"On buses."

"How long did it take you?"

She hesitated a moment. "About twelve hours."

I groaned. "You work all week as a waitress, then take a twelve-hour bus trip to see me. Pauline, that's crazy." When her eyes began to cloud over, I rushed on. "It means more to me than you'll ever know. I love you for it. I'm just afraid for you, that's all."

I wanted to take her in my arms—at least hold her hand—but all we could do was stare hungrily across the table at each other.

During our conversation about Jay Paul, her family and the operation, I also learned that Pauline had lugged the heavy suitcase of documents up the coast where she had a hearing with the prison superintendent at Tracy in hopes of speeding up my parole. Again I shook my head in concern and wonderment. What an indomitable woman! What an incredible wife!

Pauline had something else on her mind. "Jay, I've done a lot of praying lately. The Lord was very close to me when I had that operation and He has been with me during this trip. I truly believe He has a plan for us, Jay. There is a reason and purpose for all the suffering we've had to go through. That's why I made such a special effort to see you today. You do know what day this is, don't you?"

"It's Easter."

"Does that have any special meaning for you?"

"You're here."

"Is that all?"

"They're showing *The Robe* here on TV tonight."

Pauline looked at me very intently for a long moment. "What is Easter all about, Jay?"

I shifted about my chair uneasily. "It's about Jesus Christ."

Pauline's eyes were very serious. "Easter is when Jesus rose from the dead. He was resurrected. He reappeared to His disciples and turned their despair to hope. They were defeated men until this happened. After the Easter resurrection, the disciples were filled with power, Jay. Do you see now why I felt this particular day was so important to us, why I was determined to see you no matter what?"

I was somewhat taken aback by her intensity. It thrilled me that Pauline had gone to such trouble for me, but I didn't know how to respond. I stammered something in reply and saw disappointment in her face.

The bell sounded; visiting hours were over. It had gone so fast. Before she left, Pauline had one parting thought.

"Easter is a day for hope, Jay. I know you love me, Darling, but I need more than that to make it. I need to have hope for our future. I believe there is real goodness in you, but it won't come out until you let it."

Her eyes filled with tears and all I could do was hug her before we had to part.

Before going back to my cell, it was necessary to strip and be searched again. This angered me. Even on Easter a prisoner could have no self-respect. Pauline was gone and it would be a long time before I saw her again. The light in me had been turned on briefly; now I saw only more blackness ahead.

Suddenly I very much wanted to see *The Robe* again. On re-entering my cell block I asked for Cooper, my unit guard. He appeared and viewed me coldly.

"I have a special request to make, Sir. *The Robe* is on television tonight and I would like to see it."

"This is not your night for television, Robinson. Why do you want to see this film?"

"Well . . . I acted in it."

Cooper stared at me with that inscrutable face of his and I felt my heart sinking. "You'll have to go to Lieutenant Legree about this in control, Robinson. I don't have the authority to give permission for a thing like this."

At control, I showed my slip and asked for Lieutenant Legree. The fact that he enjoyed being called "Simon" indicated his toughness. I stood before him and made my request.

"This is a bit unusual, Robinson."

"Yes, Sir."

He looked me up and down for a while, in no hurry to grant my request. "You have a big role in this film. Was being a star too much for you?"

"I'm afraid so, Sir."

"Letting you see this in your own unit when it's not your television night could cause trouble with the other inmates. I'm going to grant your request, but you'll have to go to another unit to see it."

He wrote out a slip okaying my request. After dinner I reported to the adjoining unit and the guard looked at me with interest. "Yeah, we heard about you," he said and passed me through to the TV room. About thirty men were sitting in front of the television set.

I hunched down on a little iron stool in the back of the room. As this was an honor unit, the prisoners could select any program they wanted. The merits of each show that night were debated. To my relief they finally took a show of hands and decided on *The Robe*.

As the film unfolded in black and white on a tiny flickering screen, I suddenly realized that it was exactly fourteen years to the day when Darryl Zanuck had looked at my first test and written his terse, one-line memo—"Take him!"

I watched myself appear on the screen, dressed in silk regalia, strutting about as master of all the Roman Empire. Sitting there on the metal prison stool, I was a gaunt grey wreck of my former self, dressed in frayed oversized prison blues, lonely and forgotten.

As the light from the screen flickered onto the faces of the inmates around me, I recalled again the night of the premiere. Anne Bancroft was at my side. Several seats away were Clark Gable and Clifton Webb. I heard again the thundering applause at the end, could feel the congratulatory handshakes, see again the admiration in

the eyes of Hollywood's celebrities. I felt myself back there, driving
along Sunset Boulevard in my gold Cadillac with two apes on my
shoulders as excited fans pointed me out from the sidewalk.

I was seeing all this in my head and watching Caligula on TV
in a daze. I could feel myself trembling. My closing speech came
to its end. I heard Caligula saying with hysterical laughter, "They're
going into a better kingdom. They're going to meet their King."

A panning shot on the crowd of extras revealed Marcellus and
Diana as they moved toward the death to which I had consigned
them. All eyes in the crowd were watching them. I thrust my fist
into my mouth wincing in pain at the savageness of my bite, and
was surprised to see that Caligula was doing the same thing on
the screen.

A luminous brillance shone in the eyes of Diana, making them
like liquid diamonds, as she held tightly to the hand of Marcellus.
They were not afraid. A slave stood at the foot of the steps, and
after whispered instruction from Marcellus, Diana held out to him
the robe that Jesus wore to the cross at Calvary.

"For the 'Big Fisherman,' " she said. Then Marcellus and Diana
started up the steps to their death. Trumpets blared and drums
rolled louder and louder.

Someone flipped the switch and the TV screen receded to a dot
of light, then blackness. I sat for a moment utterly exhausted, my
hands hanging limply toward the floor, head down toward my
hunched knees.

I suddenly became aware of a silence in the room and, raising
my head, I saw that all eyes were directed toward me. In those
eyes were a mixture of emotions: surprise, interest, admiration, respect—most of all respect.

I straightened my shoulders and walked out of the TV room
without saying a word. Still in a daze, I moved along the corridor
toward my own unit.

As I entered Unit E, I was aware that my fellow prisoners were
staring at me, having just seen *The Robe* too. The hushed silence
continued as I walked to my cell, opened the door, entered and
heard the automatic control rack close behind me.

I looked around me at the spartan and constricting space of

my cell. Even my clothes closet in Bel Air had been bigger than this! Waves of despair suddenly broke over me, until I felt I was drowning.

I threw myself face down upon the iron bunk. The film had stabbed my spirit in a new way and I was in mortal conflict. Before I had always gloried in my role as Caligula. My acting had produced rave reviews. I had felt that it was my picture, my triumph.

But tonight—Easter night—for the first time I had seen something different. There was the look of glory in Diana's face as she had gone to her death. She had not been afraid. There was hope in her eyes—Easter hope.

Dropping to my knees on the cold, hard concrete floor beside a prison cot, my face turned upward, I gazed blindly toward the heavens above the steel and cement cell block. With a bursting heart, I felt the tears running down my face. I could taste the salt from them at the corners of my lips.

"Oh God," I prayed, "if there is a God, please help me."

For the first time a closed heart opened up a crack. The cell seemed just a little brighter and there was no question about the feeling of peace that settled over me.

21

Caligula Returns

THE NEXT MORNING when I went to breakfast I discovered a very different atmosphere. Until the showing of *The Robe* I had been ignored as an aging weakling, a nonentity. Now even the roughest, toughest prisoners wanted to talk to me. I was greeted on all sides by cries of "Hail, Caesar."

No longer was I a loner in the yard. Questions came ceaselessly about Hollywood. Had I known Marilyn Monroe? . . . What was Natalie Wood like? . . . How much did I make a week? Glances were thrown at me wherever I went, and whispers followed in my steps.

The experience I had on my knees in my cell Easter night lightened my heart for days. Something had touched my spirit as I watched *The Robe* that Sunday evening, but there was no one to talk to about it. I yearned to question Pauline. Had there been a prison prayer group, I would have sought it out. If some of the inmates had any faith or even knew about Jesus Christ, they kept very quiet about it. A prison chaplain at Tracy held weekly services for the inmates, but these were formal and poorly attended.

As a result the light in my spirit soon faded out. I became more interested in my new role as a "celebrity." Without knowing it, my walk changed from that of a stooped slouch to an erect stride. Caligula was back. My voice became crisper as I realized that whatever I said commanded respect.

184

At Tracy we could correspond by mail with only a few authorized persons. For example, I could write to Pauline and a few other selected friends and relatives. Only letters from these same people reached me; any other correspondence was returned to the sender. All letters going out or coming in were read by a designated prison official who had the authority to censor any portion of a letter by marking it out with black ink.

Each prisoner was allowed to write one letter a day on one sheet of lined paper. Every night after dinner I would write Pauline, reducing my words down in size to try and get all I wanted to say on one sheet of paper. Pauline's letters to me averaged three a week. Aside from her visits to prison, drastically reduced now that we were four hundred miles apart, letters were our only means of communication.

Not realizing that Pauline and I were about to face the biggest crisis yet in our marriage relationship, I began filling my letters with boasting statements about my new Caligula role in prison. It was not what Pauline wanted to hear. Nor was she impressed when I told her about my one-man show in the prison auditorium.

After the Easter impact of *The Robe* on the prison, I was asked to give readings in the chapel from Poe, Kipling and other famous authors. Special favorites of the prisoners were *The Ballad of Reading Gaol* and Kipling's *If.*

The success of these readings led prison authorities to invite me to do a whole program in the auditorium. About twelve hundred prisoners showed up.

The climax of my presentation was Caligula's final speech in *The Robe.* I prepared my audience thoroughly. "I want you to forget you are in Tracy," I told them. "Use your imagination. You are citizens of ancient Rome and I am your Emperor. You hold lofty rank as Senators, Tribunes and military commanders. You are gathered here tonight to hear your Emperor speak. Listen well to what I have to say, for it is vital to the health of your empire and your own well being."

I then launched into my tirade against Jesus and His Christian followers, especially Marcellus. I played upon their emotions as a pianist does upon a keyboard. I could feel my audience rising upon the crests of the oration. Their feelings were exposed now, raw, out in the open. A vibrant electric current began running through the highly charged atmosphere.

Some men rose to their feet, gesturing wildly and crying support for me at key parts of the address. When I launched into my peroration, the audience began swaying from side to side within the cadence of my words, like cobras to the snake charmer's flute. These men were no longer prisoners in twentieth century Tracy. They had been transported back two thousand years to ancient Rome. I could quite literally feel their hatred for the Christians. They were an aroused Roman leadership.

Then I asked them the crucial question: "What is your verdict?"

Absolute bedlam broke loose. The men jumped to their feet in fury, their eyes wild. They shouted almost in chorus at the top of their lungs.

"Crucify him! Crucify him!" they screamed in their frenzy.

It was an ugly moment. I was startled by the ferocity I had aroused. I was stunned by the fury of these men. For I had been acting a part; to the prisoners it had become very real.

Whistles blown by the guards rang out shrilly from around the audience. The lights were turned up to full brightness. Extra guards swarmed down to the front of the audience. It took a full two minutes to calm the men down.

Once I had become the anti-Christ figure, there was no turning back. I was an instant hero, a leader; the prisoners now hung on my every word. Even the guards showed me respect. And how I drank it up! The need for love which dominated my childhood had never been assuaged. Caligula and Jay Robinson, both hungering for adulation, had become one again.

One day a husky prisoner nearly twice my size brushed up against me in the chow line. I turned on him and became Caligula: my eyes slitted, venom poured from my mouth. The offending inmate backed away in alarm, apologizing profusely.

The one thing that did return the strutting Caligula back to a meek prisoner was my appearance in early April before the two-member parole board, generally called the adult authority. This group has the authority to free an inmate before a sentence is completed. Superintendents can't do it, neither can chaplains or counselors. Their recommendations can only influence a decision. Too strong a recommendation can even result in a reverse effect on these independent, sometimes arrogant, parole board members.

This particular board contained one member with a fearsome reputation. As a former police chief of a California city, he had acquired the reputation of hunting down criminals as if they were mad dogs who should be exterminated. "Mad Dog" was what everyone called him. Whenever he sat on the parole board, things went bad for the prisoners.

The day of my appearance came. Since I could be released after six months, I had built up both mine and Pauline's hopes that the parole board would grant me this early discharge. I figured that my new notoriety would help. Having already served four months, I set my heart upon a June release.

A dozen of us waited outside the room where the board was meeting. We sat on a bench along the wall, at the end of which was a lone chair. This was called the "hot seat," being the last stop before facing the people who would decide your fate for the next year.

I had dressed carefully, making a special attempt to appear as neat and well groomed as prison blues would allow. As we slid down the bench toward the hot seat and our interview, the tension grew to an almost unbearable level, with each man's fear feeding that of the others. Finally, it was my turn to sit in the hot seat. Then a buzzer sounded and I was called into the pressure cooker.

Inside I was shown to a straight chair placed a few feet in front of a table. Behind the table sat two board members, both men. Each had a name tag placed in front of him. I can't remember what the room looked like or the name and appearance of one of these men because my attention was focused upon the dominant force in the room—"Mad Dog" Monroe.

He sat there staring out at me through thick-lensed, steel-framed glasses with cold, unsympathetic eyes. "Mad Dog" had a great bull-like neck, and with huge hammy hands, he was completely overpowering. I felt myself shrinking and shrinking.

"Mad Dog" sat scowling; he was holding my file and riffling

through its pages. My heart sank: *He's flipping through my life.*
He flipped randomly and the scowl deepened.

He looked up at me. "This is a very confusing record, Robinson."

Do I have to explain all this over again. A cold sweat poured
from my armpits; my limbs felt heavy and numb.

"Why did you leave California without checking your lawyer
or the court about your trial?"

Lamely, I explained again that I thought I was cleared, that I
had no intention of running away, that I was subsequently in the
public eye in both Florida and New York.

"Mad Dog" stared at me coldly. "Being an actor isn't going to
help you at all, Robinson."

Desperately I described how much Pauline and Jay Paul needed
me, the hardships they faced.

"You talk as if your being in prison is somebody else's fault,
not yours, that the whole world is conspiring against you," he
snapped.

I did not reply.

"Mad Dog" rested his chin on his hands and stared at me. "You
were the star of religious films and then felt the need for narcotics.
You broke the law." Cold rejection emanated from him with each
word. When I left the room, I felt that the ground was sinking
beneath my feet. I knew I was lost.

The next day my fate was posted on the prison bulletin board.
"Robinson B5985: parole denied. Next appearance before the Parole
Board: January 1968." I had been shot down all right.

I now faced nine more months in prison until my second appearance before the parole board. It was like a death sentence. How
would Pauline take it?

The atmosphere in prison after the parole board hearings was a
wild mix of joy and anger. Those who had been paroled capered
about shouting, "Hey, man. I've been cut loose." Black fury de-
scended upon most of us condemned to remain in prison. Fights
broke out all over the place, like a heat rash on dirty skin. One
prisoner took a glass jar and smashed it into the face of another,
cutting his skin to ribbons and nearly gouging out an eye.

I found myself unable to tell Pauline the bad news and postponed writing to her for days. Finally I did so, dreading her reaction. A week went by. No answering letter from Pauline. Two weeks. Not a word. Three weeks. Now I was really worried. This was not like Pauline.

The last Friday in April the loudspeaker blared: "Robinson— B5985, report to control."

I nearly panicked. Had something happened to Pauline? Trembling I hurried down the prison corridor. Could Pauline have gotten special permission to visit me? Hardly, on a Friday. My thoughts raced wildly.

At control I was directed to one of the clerks. "Robinson, you're being transferred; forestry training—Southern Conservation Center."

When I stared at him in bewilderment, he frowned. "That's what your wife requested, wasn't it?"

"Oh, yes." I had forgotten Pauline's visit to the superintendent. "I guess I was expecting word from my wife. She had an operation recently."

"Sorry about that, Robinson. The chaplain might help you get in touch with her. Meanwhile you leave here at 5 A.M., Monday."

Three days away. Not much time to contact Pauline. Going back to my cell I asked the guard if I could see the chaplain about getting a message to my wife. Later that day the chaplain appeared at my cell. A tall middle-aged man, with a warm, quick smile, Chaplain Leon England wanted to get all the facts before he went to control to clear my request. Quickly I blurted out the salient information and gave him the addresses and telephone numbers of Pauline, her sister and her mother.

"You say that you haven't heard from your wife in over two weeks? That's usually not anything to get alarmed about, Robinson."

"You don't know my wife, Sir. I usually get about three letters a week from her."

"And you believe she is upset about the parole board hearing and that's why she hasn't written?"

"That's the only reason I can think of."

"I'll find out what I can."

It was the next afternoon before the chaplain returned. His greeting was friendly, but his face was sober. "Robinson, my news is not bad or good. I did talk with your wife's sister. Pauline and your son took a bus to Texas ten days ago."

I was dumfounded. "But I don't understand . . . why did they go without telling me?"

The Chaplain looked at me kindly. "Your sister-in-law wouldn't talk about it. She said your wife needed a rest, a change of pace."

"Did you tell her I was being transferred back south near Los Angeles?"

"Yes. She said she would pass the information on to your wife."

"But she didn't tell you where Pauline and Jay Paul have gone?"

"No. She said that your wife would be in touch with you."

An icy feeling crept over me. "Chaplain, do you think my wife has left me?" It had happened to a lot of prisoners right there at Tracy.

The Chaplain put his arm on my shoulder. "I don't know your wife well enough to answer that question. If she's been as loyal and faithful as you say she has, I think not."

As I stared forlornly at him, the blackness closed in on me again.

22

Fire Fighter

ON MAY 1, 1967, I bid good-by to my friends at Tracy, climbed into the Grey Goose and headed south. My thoughts were far from the hot smelly bus, the thirty-five other prisoners chained to me and the now familiar California countryside. Nor was I worrying about the fire fighting course I was to take at the Southern Conservation Center.

Where in Texas were my wife and son? I recalled that Pauline's mother had a sister who lived in Texas, but the name of the town escaped me. Had Pauline gone there to live? There was still no news from her.

As the bus droned down the highway, I had a lot of time to think. Something had happened to Pauline; I was sure of that. In seven years of marriage we had been so close that no more than a few days had gone by without our being in contact, either by letter or phone. Now three weeks had passed and not a word. Had she given up on me? I shifted about restlessly in my seat.

For the first time I tried to see myself as Pauline saw me. It was a shattering moment. I had been almost a total failure since our marriage. Nothing had worked for any sustained period. I had dragged my wife and child about the country for years now in nothing but poverty. What had my wife gotten out of it? First tuberculosis, then her husband jailed, then cancer.

No wonder she was fed up!

During the long bus ride I felt total despair. Pauline, Jay Paul and her family were the only positive elements in my life and now it seemed that they were gone. Without them life was futile, purposeless. It didn't matter when I got out of prison if there wouldn't be anyone waiting for me.

The Southern Conservation Center is a medium security prison in Chino, California, directly opposite the Reception Guidance Center where I was first incarcerated after my trial and conviction. The Grey Goose pulled into Chino late in the evening. As we were being processed into the conservation center, one of the men began needling me. "Hey Caesar. You're too old to make it as a fire fighter."

That woke me out of a day-long reverie. The Caligula image was still with me here in my new setting. I was 37 years old, skinny, even a bit emaciated-looking, and depressed. But a new life and a new challenge was ahead and I had better snap out of my despondency.

The fire fighters' course is tough, a back-breaker. It had knocked out or flunked many men tougher and younger than I. But if I managed to pass, I would move to minimum security conditions and much more appetizing and nourishing meals. Something deep inside me stirred. I was tired of being a failure. Pauline was fed up with my failures. I had to make it.

At the Southern Conservation Center prisoners are housed in frame barracks, each holding about eighty men, built around a large grassy area. We were contained within two barbed wire fences, but apart from that there was a surprising amount of freedom of movement.

It took me awhile to get used to hearing portable radios and having lights on at all hours. Sometimes I was awakened by the scuffling of feet as prisoners clumped through the barracks. The sound of eighty men snoring was like some nocturnal devil's orchestra. But when the course began, I was so tired at night I could have slept through anything.

I started out doing calisthenics, including pushups, situps and long distance running. Every day the exercising was increased until I would be tottering on legs of rubber. My chest would be heaving and wheezing until I sounded like a factory whistle. Sparks of light shot before my eyes as if it were the Fourth of July.

After the first week I was ready to quit. Why go on? Pauline and Jay Paul had left me. There was no reason to try. One night in a moment of complete hopelessness I decided that I had had enough of the training torture. I was at that tender point where one more setback would mark the end.

The next morning a letter came from Pauline. I stared at it a moment with pounding heart. Was this a "Dear John" letter, the type so many prisoners received from wives and girl friends saying the relationship is at an end? I was almost afraid to open it.

Finally I did, with trembling hands. Reading quickly I learned that Pauline and Jay Paul were back in Los Angeles and living temporarily with her mother. She had spent the four weeks in Temple, Texas, with her mother's relatives.

"I had to get away," she wrote. "I'm sorry if you were worried, but everything was falling apart for me. I'm back now and I'll be up to see you in prison as soon as I can arrange it. We can talk about things then. I love you."

The shortness of the letter bothered me, but those three tremendous words "I love you" fell on my parched spirit like a benediction. She still cared. Whatever had gone wrong could be straightened out.

Now that Pauline was back and would be coming to see me, I had a new incentive to pass the course. One more failure would be devastating to our marriage. So it was back to the agony of the training field; back to gritting my teeth and forcing my screaming muscles to keep going. The third week I did twenty-five pushups. The fourth week I managed thirty . . . thirty-five the following week . . . and then reached the impossible goal of forty. Every week of the training course found my body extended beyond anything I thought was possible.

At times the pain and tiredness would be overwhelming. I would be on the ground, face buried in the grass stubble, chest heaving, my arm muscles completely leadened. Then I had to force myself to make that one last desperate effort and push that extra ounce of energy into them from some hidden reservoir of strength and determination. And somehow it would happen. The extra strength came, spent muscles would function again and I would break through another impossible barrier.

Day after day I kept going when everything inside me screamed, "Quit! You'll kill yourself. This is nonsense." Yet for the first time in years I was becoming healthy.

The inmates loved to gather and watch my emaciated form at work. They would yell encouragement: "Come on, Caesar! You'll never make it, Caligula!" My agony became a major entertainment for these fit young guys, and they would bang each other on the backs and collapse on the ground in uncontrollable hilarity over my uncoordinated efforts.

As I dug in my heels and kept going, the prisoners bet cigarettes and other privileges on whether I would pass the course. Most thought I would never make it. But since those who failed usually ended up at San Quentin, this hardened my determination even more.

We were running around the track one day under a blistering California sun when the man in front of me fell to the ground suffering a heart attack. He was younger than I! As the guards ran to him, I fought down fatigue and fear in an all-out determination to complete the course.

Finally came the day of decision. Dressed in complete fire fighting attire, including a full canteen and huge boots, I had to do pushups, situps, leg raises, jumping jacks and other exhausting calisthenics—fifty of each—complete a full round of the obstacle course, and finally a mile run in less than seven minutes of time.

The sun was glaring and the thermometer hovered sullenly at ninety-five degrees. It seemed as if the whole prison had turned out to watch me complete the final test. Many bets were riding on the outcome.

I began with the fifty torturous pushups while the men who had a personal interest in my efforts began to chant aloud the numbers: "Forty-seven, forty-eight, forty-nine, FIFTY!" One by one I completed all the requirements amid shouts of support and incredulity.

Then it came time for the mile run. I lined up with the others, the starter's gun cracked and we were off. My heavy boots felt like slabs of concrete and I was already so tired I could hardly stand up. *This is insanity,* I thought to myself. *Who cares if I finish or not? Or even if I live or die?* Soon I was at the rear of the pack. It was all I could do just to raise my boots off the ground and the further I ran, the heavier they became until it seemed my feet were stuck to the ground itself. It took a superhuman effort just to keep going. Sweat was blinding me. Where was that finish line?

Some of the inmates had their watches out and were either yelling encouragement or telling me to quit, depending on which way they'd bet.

The tumult reached a crescendo as I neared the finish marker. I could hardly breathe, my lungs ached, the pain was almost unbearable, and my legs were dead weights. I felt removed from my body which I saw as a machine somehow going on perpetual motion with all the parts worn out.

At last I crossed the finish line waving my arms wildly above my head, a feeling of triumph in my soul. Then I fell flat on my face on the track, sobbing air into my exhausted lungs, muscles quivering all over.

A guard came up to me with a half-smile on his face. "You made it, Robinson. You've passed with one-thousand points—a perfect score."

When I went to meet Pauline in the prison reception room my eyes anxiously sought her out. She had on a white flowered blouse and a blue skirt. Her dark hair was tied into a bun in the back. There were deep circles under her eyes, but I was relieved to see the old warmth in them.

Again we were allowed one kiss—as we were at Tracy—and then sat across a table facing each other. The question in my eyes made Pauline smile a bit ruefully. "I owe you an explanation, Jay, but there really isn't that much to tell." She put her hand on mine gently. "I began to feel pressure building up inside me during the trial last fall."

"What happened after your Easter visit with me?"

"I arrived back in Los Angeles terribly tired. And I was really down, Jay, physically and mentally, even before I heard about the parole board's decision."

My eyes were fixed on her, searching out every hidden meaning in her words. "What was bothering you mentally?"

Pauline's eyes clouded slightly. "A number of things. I felt bad for Jay Paul. He's a lonely child. And taking him to visit you in prison up at Tracy just wasn't possible." She stopped and stared at her hands.

"What else, Pauline?"

Now she looked at me directly. "For the first time I wondered if I'd made a mistake in marrying you, Jay. Always before I believed in you and our future together. After coming back from Tracy, doubts began to eat at me. I sensed you would be in prison for at least another year even before the parole board action. And when you did get out of prison, what then? Things suddenly looked bleak, unless . . . unless somehow you changed."

There was a sudden tension in me. "In what way should I change, Pauline?"

Pauline's eyes met mine for a moment, then dropped again to her hands. She sighed deeply. "Let me redirect the question to you, Jay: Are you satisfied with yourself the way you are now?"

"No." I shifted about in my chair. "But I think it's only a matter of time until I'm making good again as an actor."

"I'm talking about *you*, Jay, the inner you, not your talent— you have plenty of that. The spiritual man—this is what I feel needs to come out of the darkness and into the light."

I was suddenly reminded of something. "A strange thing happened to me Easter night after I came back to my cell, Pauline. Seeing *The Robe* had affected me in a strange way. I think it was the look in Diana's eyes in that last scene as she went to her death with Marcellus. I suddenly found myself on my knees by my prison cot. I was crying. And for the first time I uttered a prayer that I feel was answered. I felt a kind of peace."

Tears suddenly filled Pauline's eyes. "That's beautiful, Jay. Why didn't you write me about it? It would have helped me so much more to have heard this story than how you became a big shot in the prison as Caligula."

It was my turn to look rueful. "I don't know, Pauline. I wasn't sure what it meant. I still don't know."

"Don't you see, Jay. The Spirit of God touched your heart. When you knelt by your bed, you were humbling yourself before the Lord. That's why He could come to you."

I still didn't know what the purpose of all this was, but I decided not to get into an argument over religion. Pauline was in a warm mood and I didn't want to change it. We got back to her decision to go to Texas.

"The best way to put it, Jay, is that one day I suddenly felt I had had it. Jay Paul was unhappy at school, I was unhappy as a waitress. My mother, generous as she is, was tired of having to give up so much of her life and privacy. Your news about the parole board came and I suddenly decided I wanted to seek out a new life."

"But why Texas?"

"I hadn't been there in years. When I called my aunt, she invited Jay Paul and me to come for a visit. I told Mother I wasn't sure if I'd ever return. Jay, I think I was close to a breakdown. I wasn't thinking straight at all."

"Your mother should have stopped you."

"No. It was right for me to go. Temple, Texas, is a lovely small town with lots of trees and sidewalks. And so many churches. It's peaceful and quiet. I slept a lot and then I got in a prayer group of wonderful Christians. They loved me and prayed for me. It was a healing time, Jay. I really needed it."

"If it was so great, why did you come back?"

She didn't sense my self-pity, or, if she did, she chose to ignore it.

"Because nothing worked out for Jay Paul and me. No job. No

future. Jay Paul got scarlet fever and that scared me. The people
in the prayer group didn't try to preach to me, but I could tell
they all felt my place was with you."

My feelings suddenly warmed up toward the people of Temple,
Texas.

"I think this is one way God answers prayer, Jay. He didn't
thunder at me in my sleep one night and tell me to return. But
through good people and circumstances, I just knew that He wanted
me back with you."

Pauline and I were reunited again and were now only an hour's
drive apart. My heart was suddenly lighter and the darkness had
lifted. Jay Paul came with Pauline to see me the following Sunday,
my first visit with my son in six months. Jay Paul seemed much
quieter and more serious. At first he was ill at ease with me. Later,
when I did an imitation of one of his television favorites, he doubled
up with laughter and I could tell we were back to normal.

Two days later I boarded a bus for the trip to Camp Rainbow
near Fallbrook, California. There was one big difference between
this trip and others I had taken in the Grey Goose. We were not
chained since we were headed for a minimum security camp.

After leaving the San Diego freeway, we turned east and were
soon on an isolated dirt highway which had been cut through virgin
bush, winding its way up the spine of the Sierras. From the bus
it looked like a location for a World War II movie about the Burma
Road. Actually the route up to the camp was called just that, the
Burma Road. A torturous climb up steep inclines, around hairpin
bends hanging on the lip of sheer drops into deep canyons, brought
us to the camp that would be my home.

Camp Rainbow contained wooden, hut-like barracks stretching
back among the trees behind the administration buildings. The air
was fresh, pure and pine scented, but as this was late summer, a
blanket of heat covered the camp. There was a back road out of
the camp called Turkey Road. It was also dirt, but unlike the Burma
Road, it had deep potholes and ruts.

Pauline meanwhile had been working at two jobs to save money and buy a small used automobile. It was our first car since our old Buick had been stripped on the streets of New York nearly two years before. After working most of the night, Pauline would drive up to Camp Rainbow on visiting days, bringing Jay Paul with her. Picnic-style tables were set out in the campground and we could sit at these under the trees and talk without being monitored.

The purpose of our camp and others maintained by the state of California is to house prisoner fire fighters, keep them highly tuned and available as a supplement to regular fire departments for any fire that might break out. A secondary role for the prisoners is to cut firebreaks up the slopes of the mountains—wide swaths of open land on which all combustible growth has been removed. The principle is that a fire will burn up to the break, be unable to move ahead and turn back, consuming itself.

Every morning we piled onto buses which took us out to areas needing attention where we spent long hours cutting away at the bush and moving dirt from one place to another. A crisis came the second week. Following a storm, huge waves began battering the California coast. We were quickly moved to Newport to reinforce beach property. For three days we filled bags with sand and laid them in rows along the beach to provide a breakwater for the immense waves. It was highly dangerous work; two men were swallowed by the mucky, raging water.

With the dry season of September and October came a rash of forest fires, and our work doubled in intensity. As fast as we brought one blaze under control, another started somewhere else and we were off and running again.

At one point our crew was on top of a hill. A wall of fire suddenly erupted below and came roaring toward us with the speed and noise of an express train. Trees and shrubs in its path were literally exploding into flame; the air was full of thundering noise and showers of sparks. Since the sudden combustion sucks most of the oxygen out of the air, we were soon choking and gasping, the heat searing our faces and lungs.

We turned and fled before the fire, stumbling and thrusting branches from our path. I could feel my hair being singed and the air I was drawing into my lungs felt like it was coming from a blow torch. All of us were quickly coated in black grime, the whites of our eyes staring from soot-encrusted sockets.

Soon my eyes were smarting and watering so much from the smoke that I could barely see where I was going. My feet felt like lead. How grateful I was for the toughening at the basic training center as I jumped over rocks, boulders and fallen trees, pushing my way through thick undergrowth. My hands were skinned and bloody, my fire fighting clothes torn into ribbons and blackened by the fire. But I made it over the ridge to safety, putting a wide firebreak between myself and the roaring flames.

The flames halted hesitantly at the break, kicking out in every direction like some wild dragon, trying to gain new impetus. But we had done our work well. There was nothing to burn and slowly the flames subsided.

Our whole crew had made it to safety and we stood cheering and slapping each other in triumph. It was a memorable moment; I felt far removed from the scramble for money and material things that afflicts so much of the human race as we stood face to face in victory over one of the most awesome and destructive forces in the world.

In a physical sense I was still the weakling of the crew and often other members of our team covered for me. I can remember one time that my feet had been so punished by a fast hike along the mountain trails that every inch of them was soaked in blood. Although I could hardly stand the pain, my buddies prodded me forward, taking over part of my work load until we accomplished our mission.

Although there were fights and nasty episodes among us, we became a closely knit unit, functioning well because each part meshed together. By Christmas 1967 we had fought sixteen major fires all over southern California. My body was lean and tough. I had proved to myself and others that I could serve my fellowman. Soon I would be facing the parole board again. Could I convince them that I was ready to go back into the world?

On January 1, 1968, I was taken back to Chino. My appearance before the board was scheduled for the following day. Strong recommendations for my release had been placed in my file by Chaplain Jamieson Matthias and Lucie Bird. There were letters from Pauline, her mother and sister. An agent and old friend, Gene Eagles, sent in a letter stating he would be able to get me work as an actor. But having been shot down once, I was worried. When I faced the parole board this time, I was relieved to see that "Mad Dog" Monroe was not one of them. Chaplain Matthias was there to lend moral support. The session went well.

I was later called to control and told that the board had granted me my release, effective immediately. Overjoyed I scampered about like a child, shouting "I'm free—I'm free."

And then the sky fell in.

I was called again to control. A guard was staring at a paper in his hand. "You appeared before the wrong board, Robinson."

"What do you mean, wrong board? They just freed me."

"They can't free you, Robinson. You're a special interest case; you've got to appear before at least two full members of the board."

"There were two there," I exclaimed.

"Yes, but one of them was an alternate. You have to appear again tomorrow."

"But they freed me," I said weakly.

The guard looked at me with pity in his eyes. "That decision is void. You'll have to go through it all over again tomorrow."

I was devastated. One minute free, the next a prisoner again. It was like going to the electric chair twice.

That night was miserable. I could not sleep as my mind replayed the situation. Just one more of life's blows, I thought, with a slight difference. Since my body was tougher, my mental attitude was stronger. I would not let them break me.

It was a different board that greeted me the next day. Chaplain Matthias was there again. It was his day off, but this warm, compassionate man came to the hearing anyway to offer his support. I repeated my story, stating how much I regretted my offense and the dishonest statements I made during the trial.

When I was called to control that afternoon, the chaplain rushed out and pumped my hand. "Let me be the first to congratulate you," he said. "They've set you free."

My joy and relief at his words were tempered by the discovery that this board had set my release date sixty-three days away. The chaplain arranged for me to be assigned to his office as a clerk during this period. Meanwhile Pauline had taken a small apartment in North Hollywood to prepare a home for me and continued her job as a waitress.

The day before my release I was issued a houndstooth jacket, black pants, belt, white shirt, black tie and a pair of prison-made shoes. On March 9, 1968, I got up very early, shaved carefully and said my good-bys to the other prisoners. Then I reported to control. The guard opened a drawer and handed me one ten dollar bill and one five. I was going out into the world again with exactly $15 to my name.

"You must report to your parole officer within twenty-four hours. His name is Benjamin Auerbach." He handed me a slip with an address. That was the last instruction given me in prison.

As I walked out between the layers of barbed wire, the guard checked me out of the final gate. "Good luck, Robinson. I have a feeling you'll make it."

Across the parking area I saw the old blue Chevrolet that Pauline had described as our new car. Sitting in it was Pauline and our son, Jay Paul.

We ran excitedly together and threw our arms around each other. As I stood there and hugged my little family, I was too full of emotion for speech. My debt to the State of California had finally been paid.

23

The Glass Mountain

I EMERGED FROM fifteen months in prison with the clothes on my back and $15 in cash. Through Pauline's efforts we had a rented apartment, a used car and less than a hundred dollars in the bank.

Neither of us knew whether I would be accepted or rejected by the film industry. As I looked upon Hollywood in early spring 1968, it seemed like a glass mountain. Climbing it, I would find few if any crevasses to hold onto. Any more mist or rain in my life would make the climb impossible; I'd be quickly washed again to the bottom of the heap.

The simple two-bedroom apartment Pauline had rented seemed total luxury to me. Her income of $125 a week could not support us for long. But if the climb up the Hollywood mountain seemed difficult, the prospect of my finding a good job in another field seemed even more remote.

For my first evening at home, Pauline had cooked my favorite meal: a prime rib roast with green salad and baked potatoes. When we sat down, she bowed her head and said grace. It was a beautiful prayer that moved me deeply. The food was delicious, the love of my wife and son brought tears to my eyes.

After dinner Pauline suggested we take a drive to see the changes in the Los Angeles area. We started up Sunset Boulevard, toward what is called "The Strip" in Hollywood. I remembered the elegant shops and beautiful clubs like the "Mocambo" and "Ciro's," where

elegantly dressed people went for an evening of entertainment. The
area was now wall-to-wall young people in jeans and wild hair.
Many wore headbands like Indian braves. Some carried sleeping
bags and were barefoot. I knew enough about dope to tell that
many of these kids were under the influence of hard drugs while
a number were openly smoking pot. The bizarre costumes and
makeup, the glazed eyes and blank faces of the youngsters and
the wanton behavior represented the drug culture at its height.

I turned to Pauline. "For doing this ten years ago, I just spent
fifteen months in prison. Now it's accepted." She just looked at
me; there wasn't any answer.

The next day I reported to my parole officer, Ben Auerbach, a
kindly middle-aged Jewish man. "Look at it this way," he said,
"there are two years and three months left on your sentence. You're
serving it outside of prison, on parole. To keep from being sent
back you must live a totally blameless life."

It was a shock. I had thought of myself as a free man. In reality,
unless a former prisoner is given a pardon, he is never completely
free for the rest of his life; he will never be able to vote, run for
office or exercise the full rights of citizenship.

There was another jolt: "You must take periodic Nalline tests
to determine if you are back on drugs," Auerbach stated.

"What are they?" I asked.

"The Nalline test is an intramuscular injection of a solution which
causes your eyes to react a certain way if drugs are present in
your body."

"But I haven't taken any drugs for eight years."

"Well, with the Nalline test we can tell for sure."

I could not, I was told, carry a gun or associate with anyone
who was an ex-convict. I must find employment. Once a week I
was to report for a counseling session; Mr. Auerbach would drop
in on me from time to time to check on my lifestyle. It was clear
that any real freedom was still an illusion.

The parole officer then gave me the balance of money I had
coming from the state for my forestry work. It came to $24.15.
California had discharged its full obligation to me, and considered
my total worth to be $39.15.

Gene Eagles was a ticket agent for an airline when I first met him during the height of my Caligula success. He had wanted to become a theatrical agent and I had befriended and encouraged him. Gene had not forgotten and wanted to help. He cautioned me not to mention my prison experience unless asked and said he had put me up for several good parts.

When I explained my immediate need, he nodded. "I'll do all I can. Try to hold on—something will break, I'm sure."

My first visit to the Nalline Test Center was unsettling. Located in one of Los Angeles' seamiest districts, I had to walk by dozens of winos and addicts, sitting or lying about on the sidewalks. Inside the test center were former addicts waiting for the results of their tests.

The procedure of the Nalline test was explained. First the pupils of my eyes were measured. Then I was given an intramuscular injection. After a wait of twenty minutes, my pupils were remeasured. If they responded properly, I was released.

While I was waiting for my test to be completed, two young men failed theirs and were taken out of the room through a back door to a holding cell in the basement. It was back to prison for them. My heart lurched.

When my test showed I was clean, I couldn't leave the place quickly enough. The process was repeated about every two weeks, but I never knew when I'd be summoned for this test. Sometimes the notice would give me only an hour's warning.

The weeks passed. Determined to be respectable in every possible way, I always dressed in a suit and tie, kept good hours, stayed close to my family. Yet I always felt cold chills race up and down my spine every time I saw a police car.

One night Pauline and I were invited to a party by some old friends. When we arrived I was startled to smell a familiar scent throughout the apartment. Marijuana! One young man gazed at us with vacant "gone-away" eyes, his hands hitting two sticks together in time with some orchestra that performed only inside his skull.

Panic swept over me. While on parole, I would be judged guilty by association.

"We've got to get out of here, Pauline," I hissed at her. "I could be sent back to prison for just being here."

My host overheard my remarks. "Don't be silly, Jay. Everyone smokes grass now."

Suddenly there was a loud pounding at the door. Every blow shouted *"police."* Although the apartment was on the third floor, I thought about jumping through the window.

When the door was opened, framed within it were two policemen. "Would you mind holding down the noise?" said one. "We've had some complaints from people in the building."

They were either unaware of the intensely singular smell of marijuana, or chose to ignore it.

I took Pauline by the hand and fled the apartment.

On another occasion we drove to a shopping center, parked and walked inside a clothing store.

"Jay," said Pauline suddenly, "I left my shopping bag in the car. Would you get it for me, please?"

I hurried outside, located the car and was having difficulty opening it, when a "black-and-white" cruised by, two policemen sitting in the front seat.

And then I realized that the car I was trying to open was not ours! It was the same model and color but definitely not our car.

Shaking, I hurried back indoors and gave Pauline the keys. She had to go get her own bag and I was afraid to touch the car again for days. I was literally afraid to drive for fear of having my parole revoked.

Soon I was calling Gene Eagles three times a day. I was desperate to be able to tell my parole officer I had found work. But it was a time of recession for major motion pictures and late spring was off-season for television work. Nine weeks after release from prison, when I was a basket case of anxiety, Gene got me an interview with Paramount casting director, Joe D'Agosta.

"Don't be nervous," Gene told me. "Joe doesn't know about your problems and he's a friend of mine. I think he'll give you work."

Dressed in a dark-green sweater and brown corduroy jacket, I went to the Marathon Street studio, determined to take Gene's advice. D'Agosta was a young, dark-haired man, capable and sensitive to talent, according to my agent.

"Gene told me about your role in *The Robe,*" he began. "But I've never seen the film. Tell me about it."

Something snapped in me. "I'll do better than tell you, Mr. D'Agosta. I'll show you."

Before his eyes, I became a chameleon. I could feel Jay Robinson leaving the room, and the spirit of Caligula taking over. The mad Roman Emperor began strutting in D'Agosta's office, wheedling, demanding, threatening and whining. My eyes glittered as I delivered the full final scene from *The Robe.*

Phones were ringing but D'Agosta let them ring. When I finished, I was perspiring, panting and weak.

"That's incredible!" D'Agosta exclaimed. "You'll be hearing from me soon, Mr. Robinson."

Two days later he called me back to Paramount to read for the producers of the television show *Mannix,* Ivan Goff and Ben Roberts. The show starred Mike Connors and I was given the part of a villain in an episode titled "Pressure Point." It paid $1,250 for four days work.

I was jubilant. My last salary as a firefighter in prison paid me $9 a month.

I had taken that first step up the glass mountain.

Several days later I came down with a cold and took an antihistamine to shake it off. Suddenly I was summoned for the Nalline test.

I thought it would be routine as before. The technician measured my eye pupils, then gave me the injection. I waited the necessary time and he remeasured my eyes. I was thinking of a phone call I had to make as soon as I left the building when the technician dropped a bombshell.

"You've failed!"

Shaken, I became physically sick. Scenes of prison flashed before me. What could have happened? And then it came to me. Stammering with fear, I told them about the cold remedy I had taken.

"Wait another thirty minutes," I was told, "then we'll check you again." It was the longest thirty minutes of my life.

I had made my career breakthrough; now it all hinged on a simple measurement of my pupils. If they did not measure correctly, it would be back to prison, another long separation from my family and the irrevocable destruction of my career.

I watched as another young man was taken out the back door to the holding cell. I was filled with even more horror than before.

A single lone fly buzzed aimlessly around the room. My sensitivities were so aroused I could follow its every movement with my eyes shut. A man nearby was breathing in-and-out with a wheezy-bubbly sound. An object was dropped onto the surface of a metal medical table; it sounded like a clap of thunder.

The minutes passed slowly, each an eternity unto itself, as I fidgeted on my hard metal seat. Finally, the technician beckoned me with a peremptory flick of his hand. His face was sour and depressed. I was so glued to my seat with fear that I had to put one hand on each side of the chair and quite literally push myself upright.

Regarding me with a cold, deliberate stare, the technician raised his calipers and, squinting through the eyepiece, took his measurements of my right eye. He moved the instrument over to my other eye. Sweat streamed down from my armpits. Putting his instrument down, he gazed stone-faced at me. "Okay, Robinson, you made it this time. You can go."

I stood rooted to the spot. The words did not match the forbidding manner of his delivery nor his facial expression. When full comprehension came, it was all I could do to keep from running out the door.

Back in our apartment I sat in the flowered chartreuse chair of our living room still shaken and trembling. Though reprieved, I somehow felt in a strange kind of bondage.

Something had a lock on my spirit and I couldn't shake it off.

24

Persistence and Determination

WHEN I REPORTED to the *Mannix* set for my first film role in eleven years, Mike Connors saw my tension and was helpful and considerate. So was the director. My only tough moment was when the script called for me to pull a gun. Since having possession of a gun violates parole, I handled the weapon as if it were a deadly snake.

The director stopped the cameras. "Do that with more assurance, Jay. In this role you're a man who lives with guns."

It took several takes and a great deal of self-discipline on my part before we got it right.

The day's work over, I walked out of the set looking for a telephone. Pauline needed to know what time to pick me up.

A Rolls Royce pulled up next to me; Mike Connors peered out the window at me. "Can I give you a lift, Jay? I live in the valley too."

I hesitated, not proud of our small rented crackerbox.

"Come on, jump in," said Mike.

On the drive home Mike turned to me. "I know a little about what happened to you, Jay. Want to tell me all of it?"

Mike was decent, truthful and honest. I felt I could trust him and related my whole story in capsule form. When I finished he looked pensive and very sympathetic. "It seems to me you have two courses open to you, Jay. You can keep quiet about this and hope no one digs it up in a negative manner. But you can be sure that as you become more successful, someone will break the story and you'll have no control over it."

He paused for a moment. "Your other alternative is to get the whole thing out in the open once and for all. Then it will be behind you."

My heart was warmed by this blunt, tough, caring man. "I'll think it over, Mike. You might be right."

"If you decide to go ahead, let me know and I'll line you up with a sympathetic columnist who will tell your story truthfully."

When I decided to go ahead, Mike arranged an interview with Vernon Scott of United Press International. Vernon's story about me was good. My only complaint was with the headline writer at the Los Angeles *Herald Examiner* who tagged the piece—"EX CON TRIES COMEBACK!"

Mike was right. There had been rumors and untruths circulating through the film industry about me. The article cleared the air.

Another break came on my fortieth birthday in April 1970, as Pauline prepared a special dinner in our apartment. Jay Paul was scrubbed until he shone, while the white bull terrier which we had acquired for him a few weeks before had a piece of gaily colored ribbon tied around his neck in a large bow.

Pauline wore her dark red dress and had a new hairdo. At the appropriate moment, the lights were lowered and Pauline came in from the kitchen bearing an iced cake ablaze with golden fire from a forest of forty candles.

Pauline and Jay Paul sang "Happy Birthday, Dear Daddy." I was choked up with emotion.

The telephone rang. We decided to ignore it as I made my secret wish and blew heartily at the tiny candle flames. My wife and son cheered as they all went out on the first breath.

We cut the cake and the phone kept ringing. I turned to Pauline. "I'd better answer it. It might be a job."

It was my parole officer. "I've got some wonderful news for you, Jay. I've just been told your parole has been completed three months early. You're a free man."

What a great birthday present! Life was indeed beginning at forty.

Yet the parts were slow in coming. Four days of acting on *Mannix* had netted $1,250, but then came six weeks without work. During my first full working year I earned $7,000—certainly not enough to enable Pauline to quit her job. The second year was only slightly better.

I was floundering. At home I tried to be a better husband to Pauline and father to Jay Paul, but my dark moods often spoiled my good intentions. Occasionally I caught my wife staring at me wistfully. These looks angered me for I knew she was wishing me to be something I was not. I had tried her religious approach several times, but it didn't take. I had a ready explanation for myself: we all approach life somewhat differently; what works for one won't necessarily work for another.

While passing a novelty store one day, something in the display window caught my attention. It was a six-word credo neatly printed on a piece of plywood. I bought it, took it home and set it up on my dresser. "That sums up my philosophy," I said to Pauline who was looking at me curiously. The motto read:

Persistence and Determination
Alone
Are Omnipotent

"I know you don't agree," I said a bit defensively to her. "I'll respect your beliefs if you respect mine."

Pauline just nodded. She wasn't as bothered by my motto as by the picture of Caligula which was now on the wall of our living room.

One day a neighbor whom I'll call Rachel approached Pauline and me. "Have you ever heard of Nam Myoho Renge Kyo?" she asked with a smile.

"No," I replied rather weakly. "What is it?"

"It's the heart of the Lotus Sutra of the Buddhist sect, Nichiren Shoshu of America. If you chant it, it will fulfill all your desires, make you happy and give you what you are chanting for."

I was suddenly interested. "Does it really work?" I asked.

"It certainly does. I'm a new person since I started chanting. Why don't you come to a meeting?"

"Let us know when it is," I replied.

When Rachel left, Pauline shook her head. "I don't think we should get involved with a Far Eastern cult."

"Why not? Buddhism has millions of followers. That many people can't be wrong."

"The idea of chanting for material things seems wrong to me, Jay."

"What do we have to lose?" I asked. "Right now I'm not sure how we're going to pay the rent next month and get the car fixed."

Pauline was stubbornly resistant, but Rachel was persistent. She announced that she would take us to a meeting the following Sunday night. Pauline said she would not go. When Rachel, a friendly, intense divorcee in her mid-thirties, arrived glowing with enthusiasm, Pauline suddenly changed her mind.

Rachel was as intense a driver as she was a talker and we suffered as she wheeled her small car about the streets of North Hollywood. Finally, we pulled up in front of a large house. After taking off our shoes on the porch, we were led inside to a spacious living room, nearly filled with people—perhaps thirty. Most were Americans, about two-thirds were women. We took seats in the back.

Up front an American woman was leading the group in a chant while rubbing a string of beads. She knelt in front of a table on which were two vases of evergreens, lighted candles, a scroll, a cup of water and a tray of incense.

The chanting stopped. The woman snuffed out the candles, then turned to us with a smile and said in a friendly voice, "Good evening." Then she explained that the Nichiren Shoshu sect of Buddhism had twenty million followers, mostly in Japan but many thousands in America as well. It was growing so fast in the United States, she said, because people wanted fulfillment of their desires and peace of mind. The key to fulfillment was the Buddhist chant to the scroll of the Lotus Sutra. A scroll, the candles, the incense and the cup of water could be easily set up in anyone's home.

The woman then knelt in front of the scroll. When almost everyone else in the room went to their knees, Rachel and I joined them. Pauline, however, remained seated in her chair. The people chanted and rubbed strings of beads for perhaps twenty minutes. The woman then stood up while the rest of us sat in chairs or on the floor.

"Now let's hear what has happened to all of you this week," she said.

A woman stood up: "I went to my boss and asked for a raise. He gave it to me—ten dollars more a week."

There were murmurs and polite applause.

Reported a thin, balding man: "For the first time in my life I won two races in one day at Hollywood Park yesterday. I came home over a hundred dollars ahead."

The reports continued of financial gains and greater inner peace.

"There are some new people here tonight," the woman continued. "Do you want to be a part of this big new movement sweeping across the world? Do you want more income? A better job? If so, raise your hand."

After only a slight pause, I raised mine.

"You, sir, in the back of the room—what is it you want out of life?"

"I'm an actor. I want starring parts in films or television. I was a star once; I want to be again."

"You can be. Try chanting for one hundred days. Do it for at least an hour a day." She then went on to explain the chant and how I should obtain the necessary equipment. "Remember this: you are at the center of this worship. Your needs are the focal point."

On the way home, I asked Rachel why I had to have the scroll.

"It's just part of the ritual. But man is always at the center. He learns to fulfill himself." Before we said good night she told me I could obtain a scroll at their "temple" so that I could begin chanting right away.

Pauline had been quiet and withdrawn during the whole evening. Before going to bed I asked her how she felt about the evening.

She was silent for a long minute. "It's a materialistic philosophy, Jay, and a poor alternative to the Christian faith as far as I'm concerned."

"Are you unhappy because I want to try it?"

"I wish it could be something else."

"But don't you see it, Pauline? This philosophy ties right in with my credo of persistence and determination. The chanting is a way to ask persistently for what I want. And what I want is a successful career and the good life for you and Jay Paul and myself."

Pauline stared at me for a long minute, then shrugged. "If this has to be your thing, Jay, so be it."

Her answer didn't satisfy me, but I decided not to press the issue. The following Sunday I obtained a scroll from the Buddhist temple, set it up in our living room and began chanting in front of its oriental drawings and symbols. Before leaving for school Jay Paul, now 9, stood in the hallway and stared at me. I explained to him that this was a spiritual exercise which would make me mentally stronger.

His boyish eyes blinked. "It's like prayer then, isn't it, Daddy."

"That's right, son."

Not one to do anything halfway, I began chanting two hours a day, then went to three, until my throat got sore. When a regional meeting for this sect of Buddhism was held at the nearby Embassy Hotel, Rachel insisted that Pauline and I attend. Pauline had become more and more resistant, but once again at the last moment she agreed to go.

The hall was packed with more than two thousand people. Behind a long head table filled almost entirely with Orientals, were a series of printed slogans. Most in the audience were white, young Americans. The program began with American songs, like those sung at a college pep rally. People would suddenly jump to their feet with raised fists shouting, "AAO."

I soon found myself jumping up and down like the others. The speakers told incredible success stories that resulted from the chanting. It was nearly midnight when we got home.

Pauline immediately headed for the medicine cabinet and took three aspirins. "My head is splitting," she explained grimly. Then she paused a moment. "You know how I felt tonight, Jay? Like an old black crow in a colony of sparrows."

The next morning she had deep circles under her eyes. "Nightmares all night long," she reported. "People were jumping up and down on my stomach and shouting, 'AAO.' What in the world does that mean, Jay?"

"It's like 'Hip Hip Hooray'—a cheer, I guess."

There was no cheer on Pauline's face.

But I was determined to make the chanting work for me as it seemed to for others. Whenever a part came my way, I would triumphantly attribute it to my chanting. At the end of the year my income had increased. The parts were getting bigger. Pauline was able to quit her job.

"Don't you think this would have happened anyway?" Pauline asked.

"No. The chant really works." But I didn't enjoy going to the meetings.

The second year passed. Nothing startling had happened to my career. Once I got laryngitis and had to stop the chanting altogether. Weeks went by before I remembered to return to it. Rachel was getting very irritated with me because of such inconsistency. I began avoiding her.

All this took place during the rise of the Jesus Movement of the early 1970s, beginning in California and spreading throughout the world. Disillusioned young people from the drug scene began seeking answers through every form of religion and its counterpart, Satanism. Many were becoming Christians, but the supernatural God who asked for self-denial and obedience to Him and His commandments, as far as I was concerned, asked too much. Long ago I had decided that God wasn't going to give me the success I wanted. Even Pauline admitted that this was not the way God did things.

I took up Buddhism looking for a magic answer and spent hundreds of hours chanting. Then gradually my belief in it faded, the time spent doing it decreased. Neither the chant nor the scroll had any magic answer for me, and I began to see that I didn't need this method of self-hypnosis to convince myself that I could become a big star again. I had done it once on my own, I could do it again simply through persistence and determination. Soon I stopped chanting entirely. Then I learned that Rachel had too.

In late 1970 I was reunited with Bette Davis, someone whose friendship I had valued since we first worked together in *The Virgin Queen*, this time in a film titled *Bunny O'Hare*.

The parts were coming, even though I was continually cast as a heavy. In 1971 I traveled to Honolulu to appear in an episode of *Hawaii Five-O* in which I played the part of a vicious syndicate head. While Pauline and Jay Paul were watching the porpoises and enjoying the beach, I was enacting violence and mayhem. Earlier I had played the role of an ambassador from outer space in *Star Trek* where I wore green make-up and a blond wig.

By 1972 I was in New Orleans, playing a southern crime boss in a feature movie, *Nightmare Honeymoon*. The following year I performed in *This Is a Hijack* with Neville Brand. In this film Brand threatens to throw me through the window of a Lear jet flying fast and high. My character, as usual, was craven. "Don't do that. Kill my mother instead. Don't kill me."

Then there was a role in the TV series *Bewitched* which featured a beautiful suburban housewife with a coven full of friendly witches, warlocks, sorcerers and genies. In one episode, "Samantha's Caesar Salad," I appeared as the Emperor Julius Caesar, complete with laurel wreath and toga.

At Warners I played the part of a stuttering killer in the *Search* series. Then came *Three the Hard Way* where I played an American Nazi leader who was determined to exterminate the black race by putting a sickle cell virus into the nation's water supply. Such lovable characters!

In *Planet of the Apes*, Roddy McDowell said I was one of the few actors able to be a convincing ape. "I've always liked them," I said quite seriously.

In 1973 I appeared as a deranged saboteur posing as a priest in a Woody Allen movie.

In 1974 I played an effeminate, flamboyant beauty parlor owner in *Shampoo* with Warren Beatty. I also did *Train Ride to Hollywood*, a musical comedy fantasy in which I portrayed a Dracula-type character, the "Count," complete with cape and fangs. Years before I had sung my first song in *My Man Godfrey;* now I had to perform my first movie dance, the "Dracula Drag." After that came *Night Stalker* in which I played a museum director, expert on the French Revolution and the guillotine. And there were numerous others.

Now that I had achieved respectability, I was asked to tell my story on television shows and before youth groups. Art Linkletter had me on his program and joined me in a plea to youth to avoid the horrors of drug addiction.

On one occasion I was speaking to a group of high school students. My story got their full attention. Then came some questions. One stumped me.

"Mr. Robinson, many of us in high school turn to drugs because we are disillusioned. To us the Vietnam war is wrong. And our country is wrong to fight it. We feel that to spend our lives striving for success and status and affluence is wrong, that it doesn't really bring inner fulfillment. My question: What is there to make life worthwhile when we are turned off by our society, our leaders, and even our parents?"

I spoke about how good it was to be free in a country like America, but I could tell I had lost my audience. My hunger had always been to become a big success; these young people weren't motivated toward this goal. It was unsettling and I didn't want to think about it.

Instead, I continued my climb up the glass mountain. And my biggest opportunity came with the starring role in an ABC network Saturday morning television series as a mad scientist known as "Dr. Shrinker." The show became a hit and everywhere I went children pointed me out to their parents. Some of this fame rubbed off on Pauline, who became known as "Mrs. Shrinker." Neighbor kids would come to our front door and peek excitedly inside as they engaged Pauline in conversation. "Where's the doctor, Mrs. Shrinker?" they'd ask. "Where does he keep the shrinking ray?"

But with the success of Dr. Shrinker, I again lost my identity. Fan mail poured in, all addressed to Dr. Shrinker, in the spidery scribblings of kids. And then, without warning, the Dr. Shrinker series was cancelled at the end of a year. The television research department had analyzed the Nielsen ratings and decided we were riding in second place.

And then for some reason, the parts stopped coming. Month after dreary month passed. No employment at all. I took a full page ad in the *Hollywood Reporter,* listing my credits, announcing my availability, featuring a Bette Davis quote about me: "Jay Robinson is one of our great actors." I desperately wanted the role that would put me back on top. I seethed, I paced, I fumed about the house staring at the telephone which had stopped ringing. It was useless to start changing agents again. The problem was elsewhere.

Meanwhile our savings began to diminish as if attacked by the mad scientist's shrinking ray. The months turned into a full year of no work.

Pauline and I sat in our living room one Saturday discussing my plight. Jay Paul, now 16 and a strapping six-footer, was out playing tennis. At age 46, I was at a crossroads. I had climbed almost to the top of the glass mountain only to slide all the way to the bottom.

"What has gone wrong, Pauline?" I asked after we had reviewed with alarm our financial condition.

My wife was combing her long black hair and fixing it in a bun in the back of her head. She had on green slacks and the frayed yellow blouse she wore when she cleaned house. Her figure was trim and youthful despite sixteen tumultuous years of marriage. Flecks of grey in her hair, a series of small wrinkles around her eyes and some lines on her forehead were her only concessions to being 45.

She sat down on the sofa and faced me. "You think you've lost your identity through the Dr. Shrinker role. Perhaps so. I just hope you've lost your identity as the eternal bad guy. You've played so many evil roles, Jay, your soul must be wrung inside out."

"Let's don't get into that again. Caligula is a thing of the past."

"I'm not sure he is. Sometimes I think Caligula still lives in you. At heart you are a gentle, loving man, but these roles—they do something to your spirit."

"They put food on the table," I retorted.

"Yes, they have," Pauline's voice softened. "You've worked hard ever since you came out of prison. And you really are a Boris Karloff—horrible in films, lovable in real life. But I think God has a better plan for you if only you would turn to Him. You've certainly tried everything else."

Anger rose inside me. "What is it I do that I shouldn't do? You say I'm a good husband. I don't chase around; I've stayed off drugs; I'm not a boozer; I work hard when I get a chance; I give you everything I earn." Waves of self-pity washed over me.

Pauline bit her lip and stared at her hands. Very slowly she put her thoughts into words. "I love you for what you are, Dear. But that doesn't mean I want you to continue to be what you are for the rest of your life. People are always changing for better or for worse. You came out of prison a better man than when you went in. You were physically stronger, mentally tougher. You've fought your way through a lot of situations since then, but . . ." She paused uncertainly.

"What is it about me you'd change?" I asked stonily.

"I'd like to see you able to give of yourself more. Now let me try to explain," she said quickly when she saw the objection rising to my lips. "You give your family all you earn. You love us. At times you have been helpful to friends. Yet, going way back to your childhood, there's been almost total self-absorption. I have to say it even stronger—self-centeredness. In a way, Jay Paul and I have become an extension of yourself. I think you would like to see us as a self-contained unit not dependent on other people. Since you've had to make it on your own from your teens, you've refused to believe or ask for help from a higher power. Ego gets in the way. Ego that was fed and nurtured by the Caligula role almost to the point of your destruction."

The words hurt, but Pauline's face was loving and tears were trickling down her cheeks. My anger left, but my mind still had trouble accepting. "I wish I could see it," I said helplessly.

"If only you could give yourself to people as they've given to you, Jay. My mother and sister, the couple in Florida, the nuns in New York City, Chaplain Matthias, Mrs. Bird, many others. They gave because God had touched and opened their hearts. God wants to do this to you too, Jay."

I thought back to that Easter night in prison when I knelt by my bunk. It was like a beam of light had penetrated my mind and touched my spirit. But I had quenched it. Why?

I sighed, got up from my chair, and walked out the front door of our home. I needed to go somewhere and think.

25

Sudden Change

ONE DREARY MONTH faded into the next, until fifteen jobless months had passed. As our bank account dropped through the floor, I was overcome by depression. Pauline was getting ready to look for a job. I wondered out loud to her if I shouldn't think of another career, anything that would bring in a regular income.

Pauline would have none of it. "You have a God-given talent as an actor, Jay. I won't let you give up your career. This is happening for a purpose—I just know it."

I listened but couldn't hear her words. For what purpose had I been through so many ups and downs in my life?

One day we went for a visit to her mother's in Santa Ana. Naomi fed me my favorite foods and praised my acting in an effort to lift my spirits. My despair didn't yield at all.

Before we left, she took me into her small single bedroom, closed the door, and pointed to a large ancient Scofield Bible lying prominently on her bed table.

"This Bible has been beside my bed all through my life, Jay. Whenever things get me down, this book tells me the truth and shows me the way out. When times were good, this Bible made them better. When life was too much for me, it showed me why things were going wrong and gave me the strength to carry on. Believe me, Jay, there were many times I thought I couldn't continue."

The dear old lady paused and gazed at me with a deep love in her eyes. "Have you ever turned to God in times like this?"

"How can God or anyone help me, Mother? I'm one of the lost ones."

"No one is truly lost, Jay, unless he doesn't try to look for the path home. Why don't you turn to the Lord? You've tried everything else and right now you have nowhere else to go."

"I'll try, Mother, I really will," I said, very close to tears.

Naomi took both my hands in hers and I could feel the goodness in her heart.

"Jay, this Bible has been very good to me and beginning today I'm going to pray over it every day for you. Will you pray, too?"

Too overcome for words, I just nodded dumbly, tears coursing down my cheeks. She had touched my heart. I tried to pray the next morning but then forgot about it in a few days.

The following week a call came from a friend in a casting office, Wendy Oates. "A movie we're working on called *Born Again* has a number of roles to be filled. Senators, Congressmen, VIPs. You could fit into any of them. It's a major motion picture. Would you like me to put you up for a role?"

"Would I? That's not much of a question, Wendy. I haven't worked for over a year."

"Let me try, Jay. I'll call you back when I have some news."

The movie was from the best-selling book by Charles Colson, the man dubbed by the press as President Nixon's "hatchetman in the White House" during the Watergate affair. I learned that he had turned to Christ when his load became too heavy to carry and had eventually gone to prison over the Daniel Ellsberg "Pentagon Papers" episode.

The White House, President Nixon, Watergate! It sounded like an exciting film. A part in it would certainly help.

I was asked to meet with Irving Rapper, the film's director, in his office at the Burbank Studio. Rapper was a short, dark-haired man of English birth, with the courtly manners of a European nobleman. The walls of his office were adorned with photos of stars he had directed, including Bette Davis, Fredric March, Claude Rains, Charlton Heston and William Holden. Ushering me to a seat, he regarded me with kindly, but piercing black eyes.

The discussion was inconclusive, but Rapper managed easily to interest me in playing a role in the film.

"I think there's a fine little cameo part for you as a VIP in *Born Again,*" he said. "It's small, not more than a minute on the screen. But it comes in the closing scene of the film and the audience will remember you."

"That sounds good to me, Mr. Rapper. But isn't there a more important role in the film you think I might be able to do?" I asked hopefully.

"Well," he paused, "there is the Shapiro role, but we're looking for a big name on that one."

"The Shapiro role?"

"Yes, the role of David Shapiro—Colson's close friend and attorney; it's a major role and we've had a real problem casting it. We've been in touch with some top names."

I left with the assumption I'd be offered the bit part.

The suspense was unbearable as I waited for the offer to be confirmed. We were eating very light meals. Pauline and her mother were praying for me and, as I promised Naomi I would, once again I tried praying for myself. It was a halting, pathetic "help me" prayer.

A month passed, during which I kept calling Wendy back, asking if there'd been any word. There was none. And then, one Monday, I was called back to Rapper's office.

As Pauline drove me to the Burbank Studio along the Ventura Freeway, cars, trucks and vans stretched into the distance like a flowing river of steel under yellow-tinted skies heavy with smog. A typical Hollywood day, but at least there was the possibility of going back to work!

Inside the studio lot Pauline parked the car and said she would wait for me. A cold, clammy perspiration trickled down my body as I walked to the director's office.

We exchanged pleasantries and sat down. Our conversation was drawn to the photos on his wall, particularly the one of Bette Davis. Rapper had directed her in several of her biggest hits, including *Deception, Now Voyager* and *The Corn Is Green.* Since Bette and I had retained a close relationship, Rapper and I found much to talk about.

And then, quite suddenly, the door burst open and a tall, dark-haired man rushed in, an air of determination about him.

Glancing at me, he nodded, then turned to Rapper. "What have we heard from Herschel Bernardi?" he demanded. The director looked unhappy. "Nothing, Bob. As you know, he didn't show for the interview Friday."

"Why are we having so much trouble with the Shapiro role? First Karl Malden, then Lorne Greene, Ernest Borgnine and Eli Wallach. Now Bernardi. What's going on?"

Then, taking a look at me, as if seeing me for the first time, he asked: "Who's this?"

"Jay Robinson. I'm seeing him about the VIP role."

The man stared at me, obviously thinking. "You look like Shapiro should look," he said. "What have you done? Have I seen you in anything?"

"You probably saw me as 'Caligula' in *The Robe* and *Demetrius the Gladiators* back in the '50s," I replied.

"Mmmm, yes, I do remember you." Then he turned to Rapper. "Could he do Shapiro?"

"Sure he could; Jay can play any role. He's a fine actor. But you asked for a current name, Bob." Then he turned to me. "By the way, Jay, this is Bob Munger, executive producer of *Born Again.*"

Munger continued to ponder. Then: "Well, I'm going to have to resolve this thing with Bernardi." And he was gone.

However, he returned to Rapper's office several times as the director and I visited, each time to report on calls to Bernardi's agent and the lack of a commitment from the well-known actor. On the third such occasion, Munger asked me, "Can you join me for lunch? I want to talk to you about this film."

I walked outside and told Pauline to pick me up after lunch, then joined Mr. Munger in the executive dining room. What was happening? I had come to interview for a cameo part and now was having lunch with the executive producer.

During lunch Munger told me that he was a Christian and that *Born Again* was not his film. It was, he said, the Lord's picture. He had asked the Lord to cast His film.

Munger continued to tell me about *Born Again* as I hungrily put away a small luncheon steak. "Jay, this might seem crazy to a lot of people," he said, "but the timing of our need and your appearance here today may be more than coincidental. I'm not saying anything's definite yet. I need to make some more calls. But I'm considering you for the role of Dave Shapiro. Let's go up to my office when we're through here."

In the producer's office I sat in sweat-filled tension as I listened to his end of several phone calls concerning both me and other, more well-known actors who'd been approached for the role.

Finally he put the phone down, swung his chair toward me and studied me thoughtfully. "Jay," he said, "I'm offering you the Shapiro role. Are you interested?"

Was I interested? I was thunderstruck. A major role when I had been sweating out a bit part. I accepted. Munger then called Bernardi's agent back, cancelled the offer, then called the casting director to tell him the offer to Bernardi had been withdrawn.

And then I did something completely out of character for me. I found myself blurting out the truth of my background to him— drugs, prison, the whole sorry mess.

When I had finished, Munger sat there again for a while saying nothing. In sudden, stark fear, I wondered if I'd blown the whole thing.

"That's not a minus, Jay. For this film, that's a plus. I'm certainly not saying that going to prison is something desirable under any circumstances; I am saying you were allowed to go through all those experiences by the Lord for a purpose. Just remember this— I didn't pick you, Jay. The Lord picked you, and you must thank Him."

When our talk was over, I ran down to the parking lot where Pauline was again waiting for me.

"You won't believe this, Pauline; they've offered me the second biggest part in the movie."

Pauline didn't seem at all surprised. "I know, Jay. I was expecting something like this. That's what we've been praying for, isn't it?"

When I talked with the casting office about compensation, the conversation was quite brief. "I have been instructed by Robert L. Munger to pay you what the role of Shapiro is worth," the man said. "You will receive a salary of three thousand a week for eight weeks."

My heart lurched. It was more than I could ever have expected.

". . . You are also to receive star billing; your name will appear the same size as Dean Jones who plays Colson."

I was flabbergasted. Without saying one word, I had had all my desires fulfilled. No haggling, no arguments over billing. I felt dazed.

After years of playing monsters, this was another breakthrough. I was getting my chance at last to portray a sympathetic part, a role that had warmth and human compassion. And this was only the first of a series of amazing experiences.

One day I met Dean Jones, a handsome, articulate actor who had starred in many Disney films. He walked into the offices at Burbank with a warm smile and greeted me with a hug. This I learned was the gesture that drew you into a brotherhood of love I had never known before. Not the affected superficiality of embraces which show business people give each other, but a muscular bear hug of honest affection.

As I prepared to leave, I saw Bob Munger talking with Dean Jones and the wardrobe man, Bob Scott. Munger motioned me over. "Join us for a prayer, Jay."

We stood there in a circle, arms around each other, while first Bob, then Dean Jones prayed. The gist of it was simply, "Lord, we want this to be your picture. Please guide and protect us."

The words I barely heard. Small electric shocks were shooting through me. A feeling of extraordinary warmth filled me from the top of my head to my feet. I fought back the tears.

In December 1977 we flew to Washington for crucial shots around the Capitol. There I met Chuck Colson. Again it was instant brotherhood. Colson came up to me and without any hesitation threw his arms around me as though I were a longtime brother. What surprised me, I guess, was that I was received so warmly, even though I was not a Christian.

When production started, Washington was enveloped by a sea of angry, grey clouds, and a cold, dismal December rain fell, soaking us through and through. I saw Dean Jones, his wife Lory, and several others praying. At the next break, wet and bedraggled, I asked them what it was all about. "There's a lot of tension here today with the bad weather and everything. We asked for God's protection."

Suddenly I felt peace. The weather cleared up and for the rest of our stay in Washington it was like Indian summer. The morning we left, the first snow of the winter fell in a great white curtain; a day or two earlier and this would have made production almost impossible.

Dean and I shot a scene on the Capitol steps. I had a line to deliver to Dean Jones that was strangely real. "Is it okay if an atheist like me says, 'Hallelujah'?" I asked him.

Dean replied, "In any language that means praise the Lord, Dave."

I caught a glimpse of Colson watching us, drinking in the dialogue. When he caught my eye, he tried to smile but his lips were trembling with emotion. He came up to me and without saying a word, just gripped my hand.

Later, Frank Capra, Jr., our producer and son of one of Hollywood's most illustrious directors, passed me a note. On it was penned, "Jay: You are great. Your fellow ex-con, Colson."

That touched both Pauline and me. Pauline had been very suspicious and skeptical of Chuck until she got to know him. She is usually on target in her evaluations of people, but Colson surprised her. "I was wrong about him," she admitted. "His faith is real."

One day while talking to Dean and Lory Jones, I described my life as a garden hose that had lain in the dirt for a long time; much water would have to pass through it, before it could produce a clean and pure flow.

Dean looked at me in amazement. "Why that's like something right out of the Bible, Jay."

Back in California, Dean and Lory took me to a New Year's service at their church in the San Fernando Valley, the Church on the Way, whose pastor, Jack Hayford, gives inspired sermons and teachings. During the service we were all given a piece of paper and an envelope and told to write a letter to the Lord, asking for New Year's blessings. In a moment of deep emotion, I wrote one, sealed it in the envelope and addressed it to myself. Jack Hayford promised to mail the letters back to us in sixty days. Within a week I had forgotten all about it.

Several times after a day's shooting at the Burbank lot, I would hitch a ride home in Dean's car, since he too lived in the valley. Together we would listen to tapes on his stereo system. Then we would talk about the message.

One day as he pulled up in front of our home he said, quite matter-of-factly, "Jay, it's hard for me to believe you've never given your life to the Lord. You pray with us, join in our discussions, empathize with us in every way."

"That's true, Dean. I love you guys like you were my own family."

"Then why don't you just jump in the water? Right now. Give your life to the Lord."

Something inside made me pull back. "Let me think about it some more, Dean." I hadn't done a very good job of running my life, but I still didn't want to give up control over it.

Shortly after this, another giant of a man entered my life. Former U.S. Senator Harold Hughes, three times Governor of the state of Iowa, ex-drunk, ex-truck driver, and ex-prisoner in more states than he cares to talk about, arrived in Hollywood to play himself in *Born Again*.

During the Watergate years, Senator Hughes was one of the chief critics of the Nixon administration. As a result, Colson had placed Hughes' name at the top of Nixon's "enemies" list. Years later, when the Senator became convinced of the sincerity of Colson's change, he embraced him as a brother and helped him in every way possible. Now Hughes was to play himself in the Colson story.

When I first saw this rugged bear of a man at a party in Bob Munger's home, he was being treated with awed reserve and respect as befitting a man who, in 1972, was seriously considered as a nominee for President of the United States. For a reason I didn't understand, both Pauline and I were instantly drawn to him. To us, Hughes was a rock of truth and honesty—like Peter, the "Big Fisherman" in the Bible. In that deep voice of his, Harold told me that following his conversion, after almost taking his own life, he had seen *The Robe* many times. It had, he said, been a great strengthening factor in his faith.

Several days later on the set, Harold and I had a chance to talk, and I shared with him the mess that I had made of my life. His eyes probed mine deeply.

"Jay, you need a healing from all that," he said. Then he put his large muscular hand on my head and began to pray.

Something happened to me almost at once. This strong right hand on my head had maneuvered heavy weapons during World War II, driven huge trailer trucks and directed the affairs of a state for six years. But the power I felt in his hand had nothing to do with these experiences. I felt like my head was plugged to an electrical current. Waves of power washed through my brain.

"Lord, this son of yours has messed up his life," boomed a deep voice. "He needs healing from many wounds; his body is filled with scars; his mind is filled with fear and confusion. Heal him, Lord. Cleanse from this body all impurities and wrong thoughts. In the name of Jesus, free Jay from darkness and fill his mind and heart with Your light."

The effect of this prayer was miraculous! I suddenly felt many pounds lighter. A hazy cloud seemed to *whoosh* right out of my head.

I hugged Harold. The impact of all the good men I had met in the past few months since becoming a part of *Born Again* staggered me.

That night in our living room I began reviewing these events with Pauline. "You and your mother started it all with your prayers. It's so hard for me to believe. I've asked God many times before to give me a big role in a film or a play. He never did. But you and your mother pray and it happens. Why? Does God know your voices? Does He only answer prayers from Christians? Does He listen only to desperate situations?"

"I don't know how to answer your questions, Jay," Pauline said. "But I do know that God isn't hit-or-miss in what He does. He didn't give you a big part in this film just to acknowledge Mother's and my prayers."

"Are you saying that God has some other reason for my being in this film than just to save us financially?"

"Yes."

"What could it be?"

Pauline's soft brown eyes looked at me quietly. "Only time will tell."

January 16, 1978, was not a working day for me, so that morning Pauline and I went to our local bookstore and gift shop to find a present for Bob Munger's birthday. We settled on a striking El Greco Jesus. Back at our apartment, Pauline gift-wrapped the El Greco and also a carrot cake she had made. About 3 P.M. I drove to the Burbank Studio, intending to drop off the presents and then go to Jay Paul's school and give him a lift home.

It was pouring rain—strange weather for California. When I got to the producer's office it was teeming with activity. I caught the eye of Rhonda Grose, Munger's warm-hearted and personable receptionist, and started to leave the gifts on her desk, when the producer burst out of his office.

"Hi, Bob," I said to him. "Left a couple of gifts here for your birthday."

A smile spread across the producer's face as he thanked me.

I turned to leave when a thought struck me. "Bob, do you know a good agent?"

"The best there is," Bob replied, airily, but not flippantly.

"Who is that?"

Munger was suddenly very serious. "I'm talking about an 'Agent' who will take charge of your whole life. Would you like that, Jay?"

Instantly, I knew what he meant. Time seemed to stop. It was one of those moments of crystal clarity. The confusion in my mind was gone, undoubtedly dissolved by that prayer of Harold Hughes several days before. I didn't evade the question or the challenging look in Bob's eyes. Instead a surge of joy shot through me.

"Yes," I said, "I want that."

Munger issued instructions to Rhonda that he was not to be disturbed. Then he led me into his office. As long as I live, I'll never forget the scene. It was after 4 P.M.; I sat on a couch with my back to several windows. A driving rain was lashing at the window panes behind me, darkening the office. Across the room was a large tank of tropical fish. Munger's desk was to the left. He sat down beside me and began talking.

"I want to make sure you understand exactly what you're doing, Jay. Are you ready now to ask Jesus Christ into your life, to accept Him as the Son of God and as your Lord and Savior?"

I nodded, my heart racing.

He took out a small booklet and read me the four spiritual laws which told of God's wonderful plan for His children, of His link with us through His son, Jesus, and how we receive Him into our lives.

"First, Jay, you need to renounce the evil forces that have plagued your life, then make a confession of past sins and a request for forgiveness."

"I'm ready to do that. Please tell me how."

We knelt together on the thick carpet of his office and he guided me through the various steps of renunciation, confession and forgiveness. There was only a slight hesitation when I repeated after Bob, "I renounce you, Satan, and all your work in me." How many years had it taken me to come to this point—how hard my pride and ego had fought it!

My acceptance prayer was very halting as the tears rolled down my face. "God, I want to be a Christian. Please forgive me for all the years I rejected You. Help me to be a whole man. I ask you now into my life and accept your son, Jesus, as my Savior."

Bob prayed too. "Please come into Jay's life, Lord. Give him your love and your peace and your joy so he will find true fulfillment as your new child. We thank you and praise you for bringing us together and for blessing our work."

Bob wouldn't let me go without giving me a Bible and several pamphlets to read. In fact, he ran through the rain to get one of the pamphlets out of the trunk of his car.

It was Bob's forty-seventh birthday.

It was a birthday for me too—a new birth into a new life.

26

Return to Chino

THERE IS NOTHING more refreshing than to step into a hot shower after hours of grimy physical work and feel the dirt and soot soak off and drain away.

I had a comparable sensation that rainy January afternoon in Bob Munger's office; only this time my spirit was washed clean and my heart was cleansed. Where there had been confusion and tension and darkness, now there was serenity and peace and light.

Putting Jesus Christ first in my life was not a conclusion but a beginning. Although almost 48 years old, I was suddenly a spiritual baby. Together Pauline and I began reading the Bible and various Christian books. I became a part of a men's Christian fellowship and asked Jack Hayford, pastor of the Church on the Way, to give spiritual direction to my new life.

The year had begun well. After eighteen years of marriage, Pauline and I had been able to buy the small house we had been renting. Piece by piece we were getting it tastefully furnished.

Jay Paul was a junior in high school and was planning to go to college. Tennis was his big interest.

Early in March I received an envelope in the mail from my pastor. It was the letter I had written to God during the New Year's service in our church.

It began, "Dear Lord:

"Let me see my mission clearly in the years ahead and give me

232

proof abundantly in my daily life and in the life of my family so that I may be encouraged to continue on the path. Relieve me of anger and bitterness about the past and let me fulfill at last those dreams held so long. For a higher good, let me at last truly sense my mission, purely and not for vain glory, but so that I may truly touch the lives of others."

There was a wistful longing for material success in my letter and a desire that my life might be meaningful to others. One request had already been answered with a totality that startled me: God had taken away the anger and bitterness I felt about the past. Harold Hughes' cleansing prayer had begun this healing of the old wounds and scars and the Holy Spirit entering my life in the producer's office had completed this work.

The first sign of this healing came when the production manager of *Born Again* selected Chino as the location for a number of prison scenes. This meant I had to return to my old prison, the scene of so much unpleasantness.

I shuddered when I told Pauline about it. "I don't know if I can even act in that place. It has such awful memories."

When I mentioned this to Dean Jones, he prayed with me that the tension would roll off. "See it as a triumphant return," he suggested.

During our drive to Chino, I was amazed at how beautiful the countryside and the lush rolling hills appeared. From the prison bus eleven years before, the scenery had been dull, flat and grey.

The prison buildings also surprised me. Before they had seemed huge and menacing. Now they looked well kept and merely institutional.

As we drove into the parking lot where Pauline and Jay Paul had waited for me on that day when I had been released, I was stunned by the sign fastened above the gate. "Welcome Back Jay Robinson—Star" it said, in huge black letters. Clustered underneath the sign was a welcoming committee consisting of Chaplain Jamieson Matthias, that delightful man who brings God inside Chino with him every day; the assistant superintendent, Marvin Ryer, and about twenty-five off-duty guards. I was overwhelmed.

When we began filming, I saw a large group of inmates grouped behind a barrier watching us. Their faces wore the same dead expressions I remembered so well. Their vacant eyes moved me deeply and I walked over to shake hands and offer words of encouragement. As I did, I had an inner surge of joy and an awareness that, like Chuck Colson, I too was to be a part of a prison ministry. What started off as an experience to be dreaded ended as one of the high moments of my life.

Pauline had told me in a hundred different ways during our marriage that I needed to learn to give of myself. I had not understood what she was talking about. "I try to be friendly," I had reasoned. "I give everything I have to you and Jay Paul."

But I hadn't, really. For the first forty-seven years of my life I was an island unto myself. As boss of this island, I fought off desperately anyone who tried to encroach upon it. Pauline brought the first real light into my little world, and then came Jay Paul. I made room for them on the island, but it became us against the cold world. Take what you can get and hold on to it desperately, was my philosophy. I didn't want to give anything away because I had so little.

Pauline was trying to tell me that when I held on to things tightly I would lose them; in fact, there is a scriptural injunction which spells this out quite clearly: "Whoever seeks to save his life will lose it, and whoever loses it will save it, and live" (Luke 17:33, NEB).

Yet my mind was too filled with confusion to hear my wife and as a result I nearly lost her and my son. I had, in fact, lost everything of any material value.

Where the words of Pauline and others fell on rocky soil, the new "Voice" inside me told of the richness and fulfillment that would come as I gave time and love and effort to those in need.

This same voice spoke when I read of Roman Polanski's arrest and incarceration at Chino on a morals charge involving a teenage girl. When I looked at the newspaper picture of this talented director, chills raced down my spine. I could see myself in him. As I stared at this face, I remembered two tragedies in his life: his parents had died in a Nazi concentration camp and his wife, Sharon Tate, had been knifed to death by the Manson gang while pregnant. Death, violence, hatred were the themes of movies he directed which all focused on the dark side of life, such as *Rosemary's Baby* and *Chinatown.*

I suddenly knew I had to visit Polanski in prison. With deep emotion I poured out my conviction to Dean Jones about how strongly I sensed that Polanski was bound by the same dark power which had messed up my life. "The ache in this man's heart must be enormous," I concluded.

So moving had been my plea that it brought tears to Dean's eyes. We decided that since we were still shooting scenes at Chino, we would find time between takes to see Polanski.

It happened on Dean's birthday. While the cast was having lunch in one of the prison dining rooms, several of the *Born Again* crew brought in a birthday cake for dessert. Dean cut an extra piece and put it in a napkin.

The assistant superintendant then drove us over to the maximum security section of Chino where Polanski had been placed because of the publicity surrounding his arrest. We rode past a gun tower to a plain white building; inside we passed through two metal detectors and three heavy steel doors.

Roman Polanski came from the opposite direction and also had to pass through a series of steel doors. As we shook hands I saw a small, thin, intense man, dressed in the blue prison denims I remembered so well. He had dark hair, closely cropped beard and from the look in his heavy-lidded eyes I knew he was under great strain.

The visiting room had the standard, inexpensive vinyl-covered furniture including chairs of assorted pastel colors and a metal table with a formica top. The floor was covered with a beige-colored linoleum. At one end of the room was a soft drink machine. Two guards stood by the door.

"You have any change?" was Roman's opening shot.

Both Dean and I fished out nickels, dimes, quarters for his soft drink. Soon we were seated around the table while Polanski sipped the drink and gratefully devoured the white cake which Dean had brought.

"The chaplain told me about you," Polanski said, nodding in my direction. "You know what it's like to be in here." He dropped some cake frosting on my shoe, then apologetically took a napkin and wiped it off.

"Both Jay and I have done things which have gotten us in trouble," Dean said. "We've learned how much God cares about every one of us."

Polanski stared at Dean Jones with a sense of wonderment I'm sure. Why had Dean, a busy actor, come to see him? "I'm not a religious man," he said with a European accent.

"But there's a real sensitivity in your work," Dean said. "God has given you a rare talent. I just wish that your films would do more to lift our spirits."

"My films are true to life," Polanski replied.

"Life isn't all darkness."

"It has been for me."

Dean drew a deep breath. "I dare to believe, Roman, that the time will come when you will do a film that will bring hope and faith to people."

When Polanski shook his head, I then told him about my arrest and imprisonment. I saw his eyes flicker when I described my bondage to the spirit of Caligula. He admitted he was lonely and depressed, that few of his film friends had come to visit him in prison.

As we got up to leave, I felt a sense of terrible sadness for this man of extraordinary talents. He was facing a possible long prison term. He was in many ways a lost person. I wanted to pour out my heart to him. "Don't be defeated by this," I said. "I know many things have gone wrong for you, but there is a lot of good in this world. Many people do care. God cares. It took me almost forty-eight years to learn this. He can help you find peace and joy and love and meaning in this life." I stopped a bit surprised at my outburst—and unsure of myself in this new role.

Both Dean and I hugged him as we said good-by. There was a

mist in his eyes. "I'll never forget you for this visit," he said in a low voice.

The next day Polanski was released from prison and ordered to report the following Monday for sentencing at the Santa Monica Superior Court. It was the same courtroom in which I had been sentenced. Again I could identify with him, sense the agony he felt over loss of freedom, the fear of prison. I prayed for him.

Monday morning Pauline and I drove to the Santa Monica Courtroom to be on hand for the sentencing, to let him know that we cared.

He did not appear.

The afternoon paper had the headline: "Polanski flees country."

He had flown to Paris the night before, skipping bail and ducking out on his court appearance.

I ache for him. He has run from a prison sentence, but he can't run away from himself. In some ways he is still a prisoner wherever he may go. I continue to pray for him in his darkness as people once prayed for me in my darkness.

I tried to be lord of my life. It brought me bondage; God freed me. And now He is showing me that I need have no fear of anything when I'm in His love, that I can trust Him to run my life.

The ghost of Caligula has been laid to rest. Had I been possessed by the evil spirit that had driven the mad Emperor to his destruction so long ago? I don't know. But whatever force led me deep into the pit has been overcome by the love and power of Jesus Christ. Caligula no longer can infect my life or my home.

Jesus is my light now, not the lights of sound stages. God is my hope and my reason for existing, not ego and blind ambition. My eyes are fixed now, not on the pain of things past, not the difficulties of things present, as they were for so many long years, but on the eternal promise that everything works for good for those who love and serve the Lord.

Epilogue

FOR WEEKS THE sound of hammering has filled our small San Fernando Valley house. Since the cracked plaster walls were beyond restoration, Pauline and I had decided to repanel it completely.

The surprising element was that we would do it ourselves—I, who barely knew how to hold a hammer! But we were discovering the fun of it as a family project. Pauline, Jay Paul and I went down to the lumber yard, chose the paneling and then studied the instruction book.

Jay Paul, now over six feet tall and a husky one hundred seventy-five pounds, helped carry heavy panels into location with Pauline surveying their placement. I hammered the nails, more often hitting my thumb. But we were all amazed at our progress. We found that if we carefully followed the instructions just as they were given in the manual, the work went well and the finished job was beautiful.

As we worked I thought how similar this was to the Bible. All our instructions for life are right in it. If we followed its directions just as they are given, our lives would work out well.

Installing the paneling took a lot of sweat and strain. But in it I found satisfaction and fulfillment. As I labored, I thought of a fulfillment of a much deeper kind through working with Chuck Colson in the Prison Fellowship program. How well I understood the prisoners' worries and hang-ups as I worked in helping them find the source of all light. Again, I am spending much time behind bars, but now I go with joy. It was as if I had been put through the whole prison ordeal to be able to relate to these men as a true brother.

I thought of my baptism a month before at our church. It had taken place in front of the congregation, in the baptizing pool behind the pulpit. With Pauline and Jay Paul and Dean Jones nearby, Pastor Hayford had asked me again to repent of my past life and confess Jesus as Lord and Savior. I did and was then lowered into the water.

I came up glowing and joyous, my heart filled with love for all these people. The pastor said that I had left "the old man" in the water. I believed him. Not only did I feel lighter, I felt like I had wings.

All this was a far cry from my old days of living in the shadow of Caligula. I thought of the mad emperor as I pounded in another nail. Only a few nights before I had given my witness before the congregation of a local church. After I finished, the pastor asked me to present my closing speech from *The Robe.*

I shook my head. I well remembered the evil in those words and would never forget the near prison riot it brewed. But the pastor pressed and many in the congregation called out for it.

So I stood before the altar and huge cross and faced the people, praying inwardly. Within me surged a strong assurance from the Holy Spirit that He would be with me.

As I launched into the speech, I noticed something strange. The evil in it was gone! I felt completely different from when I had last given it in prison.

Now it had been cleansed. Now it was a witness to Christ and to the legions of Christian martyrs who had given their lives for Him.

"Jay?" It was Pauline bringing me back to the present as she patiently held up a wall panel for me to secure. Finally, we finished all the rooms.

As we all stood admiring the new interior of our little house, Pauline asked, "Where is the picture?"

I thought for a moment. "Which picture?"

"The painting of you as Caligula. The one you've held on to all these years."

I puzzled for a moment and then remembered. It had been on our living room wall. But when we started the paneling, I had taken it down.

"Oh," I said, "I put it into the closet."

I decided to leave it there. It doesn't mean anything to me now. Perhaps someday I'll put it up again, not as a trophy, but as a reminder of what life can be like without the presence of Jesus Christ.

Afterword

SEPTEMBER 24, 1978 WAS an important date for me. This was the night of the premiere of the film *Born Again* in the Kennedy Center's Eisenhower Theatre. Since *Born Again* was the story which included that traumatic period of my life when I was an assistant to President Richard Nixon and later went to prison for an offense committed in this work, it seemed right that the premiere of this film should be held in the nation's capital.

But this date and premiere were even more important to another man. His name—Jay Robinson. Jay was introduced to the eleven hundred premiere guests that evening as one of the stars of *Born Again;* he played superbly the role of my feisty, tenacious lawyer David Shapiro and later won critical acclaim for it.

As I watched Jay Robinson stand up and wave to that Washington, D.C. audience, I knew something of the tumultuous thoughts going through his mind. For it was exactly twenty-five years ago to the day—September 24, 1953—that Jay felt wash over him the enthusiastic applause of a Hollywood premiere audience for his remarkable performance as Caligula in *The Robe*. His role as the mad Roman Emperor, labeled by the New York *Times* as one of the ten best performances in the history of films, nearly destroyed him.

Highlights of the wild, improbable twenty-five years between premieres had to be flashing through Jay's mind that September night.

Jay and I have several things in common. We have known what it is to be on the mountaintop of success—and in the valley of defeat. A few months ago Jay and I undertook a mission together, not the first of its kind. As a part of Prison Fellowship's concern for men and women behind bars, we visited one of the oldest and toughest prisons in America at Canyon City, Colorado. As Jay and I walked between rows of small, dimly-lit, cave-like cells inside this prison, we both fought down painful memories. We didn't talk because it wasn't necessary. There were the foul, pungent odors and the shrill, clanging sounds of steel meeting steel as closing gates shattered the silence. The unsmiling faces we saw were like faces out of our past. He and I had both been there. He had never forgotten just as I could not.

Minutes later we were standing before a packed chapel. Many of the denim-clad inmates, particularly in the back rows, stared at us with suspicion, waiting for the one slip that would allow them to turn the evening into a debacle. I stole a glance at the well-dressed man at my side; Jay is now in his late forties. He might have been a banker or businessman.

I was introduced by the prison chaplain and stood before the skeptical audience. "How many of you men remember the movie *The Robe?*" I asked. Hands sprang up all over the room.

"Remember Caligula, the mad Emperor who persecuted the Christians?"

Shouts of approval and even applause rippled through the crowd. Caligula was evil. Inmates worship tough guys, the tougher and meaner the better.

"Well, here he is."

With that, Jay Robinson, fabled star a quarter century ago and now making his comeback, began speaking. It was not the kind of audience film stars are accustomed to. He spoke haltingly at first, his voice low, then confidence came. He told about the Hollywood glamour, the lavish drunken parties, the beautiful women, and his growing need for drugs. This brought understanding nods, particularly from younger inmates.

Every eye was riveted on Jay. No one stirred through the telling of his amazing story: the touching romance with Pauline, the months in prison, the struggle to regain self-respect and acceptance, and the heroism of a remarkable woman who battled the forces of evil in her husband's life. Then came the poignant moment of Jay's spiritual transformation. Some men were weeping at the end.

The inmates sensed in Jay Robinson the keenly sensitive spirit I felt the first time I met him. At the end of our talk to the prisoners, I invited to pray with us any who wanted to know the Person who makes the impossible happen in our lives. The men in the back rows were the first to respond, then others followed throughout the room. A light began to glow in one of the darkest places I have ever been.

The Comeback is the absorbing story of a man who came out of the darkness into the light, a man who has not only come back, but has come home.

I thank God for him.

Charles W. Colson
December 16, 1978

Acknowledgments

To Bette Davis—my friend in the worst of times, my friend in the best of times; God bless you.

To Chuck Colson—the man who first brought this story to the attention of Chosen Books and whom I learned to love in Christ in such a special way.

To the editorial staff at Chosen Books—Len LeSourd, Catherine Marshall, John and Tib Sherrill, Dick Schneider and Gordon Carlson, who helped in so many ways.

To Frank Capra, Jr.—for his encouragement to proceed with the writing of the book.

To Frank Neill—an old and valued friend at Twentieth Century Fox who, along with Eric Hoffman, was so helpful in compiling the photographs included in *The Comeback.*

To members of the Hollywood Press Corps—especially those who wrote favorable and encouraging stories during the past ten years. Without their support, life would have been even more lonely.

To my new friends in Christ—Harold Hughes, Bob Munger, Dean and Lory Jones, Paul and Karen Temple, Bob and Barbara Kirchner and the partners in the film *Born Again;* their love and devotion to Christ give me more strength and incentive to live for Him.

Stage, Screen and Television Appearances
of the Author

The Shop At Sly Corner, Booth Theatre, Opened Jan. 18, 1949, New York City
Gayden, Plymouth Theatre, Opened May 10, 1949, New York City
As You Like It, Cort Theatre, Opened Jan. 26, 1950, New York City
Buy Me Blue Ribbons, Empire Theatre, Opened Oct. 17, 1951, New York City
Much Ado About Nothing, Music Box Theatre, Opened May 1, 1952, New York City

MOTION PICTURES

The Robe, 20th Century Fox, 1953
Demetrius And The Gladiators, 20th Century Fox, 1954
The Virgin Queen, 20th Century Fox, 1955
The Wild Party, United Artists, 1956
My Man Godfrey, Universal, 1957
Bunny O'Hare, American International Pictures, 1971
Nightmare Honeymoon, M.G.M., 1972
Everything You Always Wanted To Know About Sex, United Artists, 1973
This Is A Hijack, Fanfare Films, 1973
ThreeThe Hard Way, Allied Artists, 1974
Train Ride To Hollywood, Taylor-Laughlin Dist. Co., 1974
I Wonder Who's Killing Her Now, Cinema Arts, 1974
Shampoo, Columbia Pictures, 1975
Born Again, Avco Embassy, 1978

TELEVISION APPEARANCES
(Titles of episodes in parentheses)

1968

"Mannix" (Pressure Point)
"Star Trek" (Elaan Of Troyius)
"The Wild Wild West" (The Night of The Sedgewick Curse)
"Judd For The Defense" (Visitation)
"My Friend Tony" (Encounter)

1969

"Bewitched" (Samantha's Caesar Salad)
"Mannix" (The Search For Darrell Andrews)

1970

"Bewitched" (The Phrase Is Familiar)
"The Men From Shiloh" (Lady At The Bar)
"Mannix" (Overkill)

1971

"Hawaii Five-O" (Cloth Of Gold)
"Room 222" (Hail And Farewell)
"O'Hara, U.S. Treasury" (Operation: White Fire)

1973

"She Lives!" A.B.C. Movie Of The Week
"Mannix" (Trap For A Pigeon)
"Search" (Ends Of The Earth)

1974

"The Waltons" (The Breakdown)
"Planet Of The Apes" (Tomorrow's Tide)
"Mannix" (Picture Of A Shadow)
"Banacek" (Now You See Me—Now You Don't)

1975

"The Waltons" (The House)
"Barney Miller" (The Sniper)
"Bronk" (Julia)
"Harry O" (Group Terror)
"Night Stalker" (Chopper)
"Doc" (Quartet)

1976

"The Waltons" (The Comeback)
"Phyllis" (A Man And A Woman . . . And Another Woman)

1977

"The Kallikaks" (Swami, How I Love Ya)

1978

"A.E.S. Hudson Street" (Shut Down)
"Flatbush" (Voodoo)

TELEVISION SERIES
(Continuing roles)

"Krofft Super Show" (Dr. Shrinker) A.B.C. Series Sept., 1976 . . . Sept., 1977
"Krofft Superstar Hour" (Lost Island, and Horror Hotel) N.B.C. Series, 1978
"Cliffhangers" (Secret Empire) N.B.C. Series, 1979

RECORDINGS

Richard III, Folkways Records, 1964
Othello, Folkways Records, 1964
Hamlet, Folkways Records, 1964